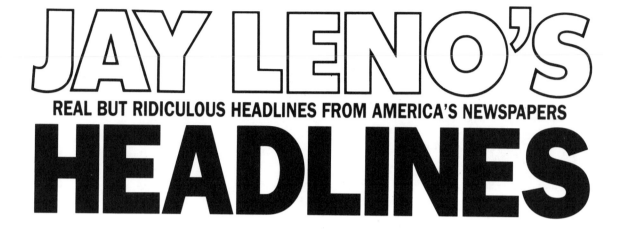

JAY LENO'S

REAL BUT RIDICULOUS HEADLINES FROM AMERICA'S NEWSPAPERS

HEADLINES

BOOKS I, II, III

COMPILED BY JAY LENO

WINGS BOOKS
NEW YORK • AVENEL, NEW JERSEY

All author royalties will be donated to the Samuel Jared Kushnick Foundation, which funds pediatric A.I.D.S. programs and pediatric immunology research.

Original book design by Giorgetta Bell McRee
Revised book design by Bill Akunevicz Jr.

This edition contains the complete and unabridged texts of the original editions.

This 1992 edition is published by Wings Books, distributed by Outlet Book Company, Inc., a Random House Company, 40 Engelhard Avenue, Avenel, New Jersey 07001, by arrangement with Warner Books.

Printed and bound in the United States of America

Library of Congress Cataloging-in-Publication Data

Leno, Jay
    [Headlines]
    Jay Leno's headlines.   Books I, II, III.
        p.   cm.
    1st work originally published: Headlines. New York : Warner Books, c1989.
    2nd work originally published: More Headlines. New York : Warner Books, c1990.
    3rd work originally published: Headlines III. New York : Warner Books, c1991.
    ISBN 0-517-08238-1
    1. Newspapers—Headlines—Humor.   2. American wit and humor.
I. Leno, Jay. Headlines. 1992.   II. Leno, Jay.   More headlines. 1992.
III. Leno, Jay. Headlines III. 1992.   IV. Title.   V. Title: Headlines.
PN6231.N63L46 1992
081—dc20
                                                                        92-6552
                                                                          CIP

8 7 6 5 4 3 2 1

HEADLINES

COMPILED BY JAY LENO

WITH PHOTOGRAPHS BY GARY BERNSTEIN
AND CARTOONS BY BOB STAAKE

1

INTRODUCTION

"Obviously, a man's judgment cannot be better than the information on which he has based it."

—Arthur Hays Sulzberger

The reason these headlines appealed to me is because they were never intended to be funny in the first place. That they're checked and rechecked by a proofreader makes them funnier still. Sometimes the humor is tinged with disbelief. I'll pick up my family newspaper, for example, and see the headline, "CONDOM INDUSTRY SLOW AFTER BIG GROWTH," and wonder, "Am I the only person in the world who noticed that?"

In this book we've deliberately avoided using headlines from tabloid or so-called "pulp" newspapers because the double entendres found in them are often intentional. It's when they're not but show up anyway in the local gazette, that you have to laugh. In the same way that a joke is funnier in church, a silly headline seems even sillier when it appears in a respected "organ of the people."

I'd like to thank the viewers of *The Tonight Show* who contributed the headlines that appear here and have made it possible for me to donate all author proceeds to charity. To them and to all of you who are encountering these headlines for the first time: Enjoy the laughs!

Jay Leno
New York, August 1989

One advantage a newspaper reader has over someone who watches television or listens to the radio is his ability to go directly to the stories that catch his eye—those stories that contain the most pertinent information. A good newspaper will offer not just information on the events of the day, but also...

LITTLE-KNOWN FACTS

Screwdrivers were made to tighten, loosen screws

Although it appears that one or two screwdrivers should be enough for a household without any confirmed do-it-yourselfers, even the unhandiest of families needs several of them.

Liquor sales dip blamed on less drinking

Criminal groups infiltrating pot farms

Criminal groups involved with drugs? Is nothing sacred?

Researchers call murder a threat to public health

How long did this study take? Do you think it was more than ten minutes?

Bush gets briefing on drought; says rain needed to end it

This is the kind of no-nonsense, put-your-reputation-on-the-line problem-solver we need in the White House.

Living together linked to divorce

'Nuff said.

Boys Cause As Many Pregnancies as Girls

?

Tribal council to hold June meeting in June

Cherokee Nation of Oklahoma Tribal Council will hold its regular June meeting at the Jay Community Building at 9 a.m., Saturday, June 11. Following the coun-

Yes, but when is the August meeting?

Some students walk others ride to school

Think this was a slow news day?

DEATH ENDS FUN

Kinda says it all, doesn't it?

9

HIGHLIGHTS

12:01 a.m. ⓫ **1988 Crusade for Children**
Annual fund-raiser to benefit handicapped children in Kentucky and Indiana. (Continues until it ends.) ⟵

Unless, of course, it's over sooner.

Toxic waste tour planned

LANSING — A citizens group began a tour of Michigan on Monday to visit some of the state's worst toxic waste sites

If you choose Chicago, may I suggest Wacker Drive?

13

Daytona Beach
VACATION for TWO
ONLY $60
at the Beautiful Whitehall Inn

| 3 DAYS 2 NIGHTS $60 Per Couple | 7 DAYS 2 NIGHTS $205 Per Couple |

Hope it doesn't rain!

In the last few years there's been a perception that Americans are soft on crime, that we're coddling criminals, that we're not dealing with them harshly enough. This next set of headlines may dispute those claims...

CRIME AND PUNISHMENT

'Shoot to stop' ordered for fights

And if that doesn't work, try talking to them.

Police use tear gas, SWAT team, battering ram, stun gun to oust woman, 65

What would they have done if her father was at home. They would have needed a tank!

Window found open

Warrenton police are investigating an attempted breaking and entering which occurred Thursday at the Animal Care Clinic at 657 Falmouth St.

When Officers ███████████ and ███████████ responded at 4:11 a.m. after an alarm went off, they found a rear window had been partially pried open, said Chief ███████████.

No one was at the scene, nor was access gained to the building, he said.

Boy, there's nothing like old-fashioned police work.

Cockroach Slain, Husband Badly Hurt

Reuters

Tel Aviv

An Israeli housewife's fight with a stubborn cockroach put her husband in the hospital with burns, a broken pelvis and broken ribs, the Jerusalem Post newspaper reported yesterday.

This sounds like the plot of a Japanese monster movie.

Slayings put end to marriage

You think it's the cockroaches again?

"First step on that long road to rehabilitation" department:

Man admits killing violated probation

A city man found guilty of a 1984 execution-style murder admitted in federal court Tuesday that the conviction violated his 1983 federal probation on a drug charge.

Animal unit seeks rabbit witnesses

Gee, don't you think *one* rabbit witness would be enough?

City outlaws giving out phone numbers, addresses of police

Solves the problem of trying to find a cop when you need one.

"I don't know how they're getting back on the streets" department:

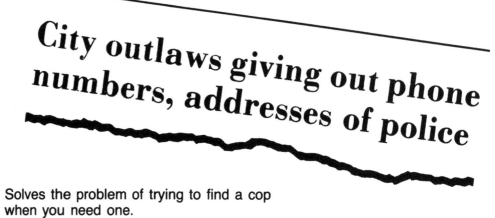

Jail's $34-million price tag doesn't include cell doors

Associated Press

JACKSONVILLE — A $34-million contract to build a new five-story jail lacks one major item — cell doors.

"It sounds to me like we're buying a car without the two front wheels. I thought when we voted to go ahead with the jail that it would come complete with doors," City Council member ▮▮▮▮▮▮▮ said Thursday.

4 Do you think you can get something for nothing? Are you always looking for a free lunch? Do you believe you can get more than what you pay for? Here are some bargains that will force even the most jaded to exclaim:

WHAT A DEAL!

Reprinted from Design News, Feb. 2, 1989 © Cahners Publishing Co.

Design a safe nuclear power plant and win $500.   Page 24

Here's a way to earn extra money in your spare time.

Step into *joyce*

Genuine fake eelskin

Don't be fooled.
Accept only imitations.

Boy, my mouth is watering already...

23

This is the guy who should be building that nuclear power plant. He uses real nails!

A breathtaking view? Good, I'm tired of looking at that dumpster.

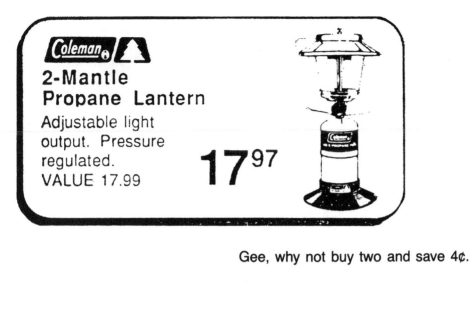

Coleman 🌲
2-Mantle
Propane Lantern
Adjustable light
output. Pressure
regulated.
VALUE 17.99

17⁹⁷

Gee, why not buy two and save 4¢.

Petland ALIVE
PUPPIES & KITTENS

LARGE SELECTION OF AKC and CFA REGISTERED
VETERINARIAN CHECKED AND PETLAND
GUARANTEED—   YOU ADD THE LOVE!

- Schnauzer - Afgan
- Cocker   - Cairn
- Maltese   - Dachsund
- Yorkie   - Lhasa
- Shih Tzu   - Bichon Frise

- Siamese
- Oriental Short Hair
- Himilayan

The first rule of merchandising: convince the buyer that
your product is superior to the competition. For example,
notice that this store is selling *alive* puppies and kittens.

Hmmm...
100% off.
But does it have
a breathtaking
view?

New
math?

STOCK UP AND SAVE!
78¢ EA. SOFT WHITE **LIGHT BULBS**
• CHOICE OF 60, 75, OR 100 WATTS. (LIMIT 2 BULBS PER CUSTOMER.)

Rather than make two trips of one bulb each, why not stock up?

Hey, weight watchers, without the ingredients it's zero calories.

CLUB CAR GRILL
Our Reg. Steak
SANDWICH
2 for only $2⁹⁹
(Ingredients extra)

White Flower Two Day Sale

FRIDAY ONLY

"Boy, am I hungry" department:

BUY ONE GET ONE FREE 14 lb. CHEESEBURGER

1 Coupon
Per Customer
Per Visit.

This coupon
not valid with
other specials.
With Coupon.
TVF.
Offer Ends
2/28/87

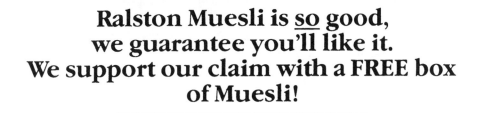

Ralston Muesli is <u>so</u> good, we guarantee you'll like it. We support our claim with a FREE box of Muesli!

Dear Ralston:

I didn't enjoy it. Thank you for sending me more.

Yours truly,
Jay Leno

The best things in life are FREE and here's how to get them!

SEND CHECK OR MONEY ORDER TO:

HOME VALUE COUPONS

"Nutri/System,ᴵᴺᶜ you lightened my life!"

Delicious food and personal counseling, helped ▬▬▬▬ lose 50 lbs. on the NUTRI/SYSTEM® Weight Loss Program.

The NUTRI/SYSTEM comprehensive *Flavor Set-Point*™ Weight Loss Program includes:

- *Personalized Weight Loss Profile*™ to identify your personal weight loss problem.
- A variety of delicious meals and snacks.
- One-on-one personal counseling.
- *Behavior Breakthrough*™ Program for long-term success.

Our client, lost 50 lbs.

Don't Wait, Call Today.

Of course she lost weight. They cut her hand off! She can't feed herself!

First they cut off their hands, then they shrink them!

Let Nutri/System help get you ready for the Holidays

▬▬▬▬ lost 30 pounds and 25½ inches.

"It was the easiest program I've ever been on. It works!"

"Thanks Nutri/System"

1 SOUND AND THE TIME PROJECTS ON THE CEILING
No need to turn on a light, squint your eyes, wake the
spouse. In fact, all you need to do is just cough, clap
your hands, whistle, speak...and our sound-activated
clock projects the exact time on your ceiling! Features
alarm and hourly chime mode; easy-read LCD display.
4″x3″. Batteries not included. Assorted, let us choose.
G531491 — Clock.....................~~$15.99~~; SALE $9.88

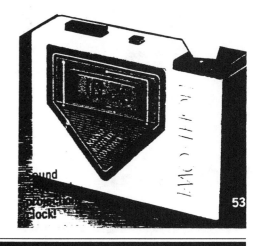

And what is your spouse doing while you're coughing,
clapping your hands, whistling, and speaking?

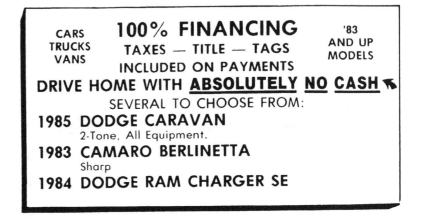

I like a guy who says what he means.

FORECLOSURE LISTINGS

Entire state of NJ available. Deal directly with owners. 5-8 months before auction. Call 201-286-1156

The entire state of New Jersey. What a deal!

As was stated at the beginning of this book, none of this material was gathered from tabloid-type newspapers that deal in lurid, sleazy, sensational headlines, e.g., ELVIS SEEN PLAYING POKER WITH DOG. No, our sources are ordinary newspapers— ones meant to be read by the entire family. So if you see Grandma drop her tea, Junior pick up a paper with a hole in it, or Mom complain because there's an entire section missing, the following headlines could be the reason why...

PLEASE CANCEL MY SUBSCRIPTION

Condom Week starts with a cautious bang

In 1968, a California pharmacist recommended to then-Governor Ronald Reagan that the California public be educated on the use of condoms to halt the spread of sexually transmitted diseases.

The public education tradition continues. Today marks the first day of National Condom Week, and UI Student Health Services does not plan to let the week go by unacknowledged.

Condom plant pulls out; was there a leakage?

Albany blew it again!

A Japanese condom manufacturer actually planned to come to Albany.

Okamoto Industries, of Ibaraki, Japan did their homework on Albany, the Good Life City before enplaining for the U.S.

Condom firm stretches product line

'We may be addressing the ego for many men, but on the other hand, it may be the only way to get them to use condoms.'
— Maxx creator David Mayer

Now, for the man who has everything, or at least thinks he does, there's Maxx, the condom that's 25 percent larger than most.

California motorists carefully clean up condom spill

CORTE MADERA, Calif. (UPI) — A box containing about 5,000 condoms fell off a truck and scattered over a busy freeway, halting two lanes of traffic for a half-hour, the California Highway Patrol said.

Cookies with condoms fail family-taste test

MILWAUKEE (AP) — A record store that sold fortune cookies containing miniature condoms as a joke failed to draw a laugh from officials in charge of the city's largest summer festival.

'Chitlin' truck loses load in Climax

By Climax Reporter

Chitterlings arrived a few weeks early for Swine Time when an accident occurred involving an 18-wheeler tractor trailer rig carrying about 2,000 pounds of livestock (mostly hog) intestines and body parts, which are used in pet food, and a car (unknown in make or model) Nov. 1 at approximately 9 p.m.

From the "Your mother always told you to wear clean underwear" department:

Leave trousers behind for single's party fun

Staff Writer

It's every man's nightmare — you're at a party with beautiful women, you feel well-dressed, but suddenly you realize you're not wearing any pants.

This dream came true for about 600 single people at the Lafayette Hilton Ballroom last week, and it wasn't as bad for the men as it would seem. In fact, the third annual Boxer Shorts and Mini Skirts Party "For Singles Only" was a big success.

From the "Use it or lose it" department:

Rangers to Test Peeters for Rust

Capitals Goalie Makes 1st Start Since Feb. 17 Tonight

Pete Peeters owns the classiest goaltending statistics in the National Hockey League. He also has a medical record that has kept trainer Stan Wong gainfully employed during this season of minimal injuries for the Washington Capitals.

Lebanese chief limits access to private parts

BEIRUT, Lebanon (AP) — The military chief and head of the Christian Cabinet moved to reduce the power of private armies Sunday by ordering a ban

From the "Hear no evil" department:

Scientists Note Progress in Herpes Battle; Ear Plugs Recommended

From Our Wire Services

Scientists are making progress in battling genital herpes, a viral infection that was chipping away at casual sex before AIDS came along.

In one recent vaccine trial involving 161 sexual partners of type 1 (which causes oral herpes, or cold sores), had some protection against type 2 infection.

One drug that has shown promise in treating existing herpes lesions is acyclovir, called Zovirax by manufacturers Burroughs-Wellcome. Ongoing studies of the drug's effectiveness and

Health Watch

Ear Plugs Plugged

Ear specialists have a vision of a new health fad, and they'll give you an earful on it.

who work with jackhammers or jet planes.

Overexposure to noise is the most common preventable cause of hearing loss in the United States, says the academy in a new booklet.

Constant exposure to busy traffic, loud office machinery or even fic can have the same impact. can a couple hours next to a cha saw or pneumatic drill.

For more information, tl leaflet, "Noise, Ears and Hearii Protection," is available. Send stamped, self-addressed busine envelope to the academy at 11(Vermont Ave., N.W., Suite 30

37

Trees can break wind

Wind can be a major factor in increasing the heating bill in winter. A natural way to curb the wind is with trees used as a windbreak.

Man accused of excessively 'passing gas'

"Good thing he wasn't in the smoking section" department:

Gas smell diverts flight, but it was just passenger's pants

FORT MYERS, Fla. (AP) — The pilot of a Braniff Airways flight made an emergency landing and all 47 passengers slid down chutes after people smelled gasoline on board — but the odor was later traced to a man's pants leg.

Yellow snow studied to test nutrition

Associated Press

SAVAGE RIVER, Alaska — Biologist Mark ▓▓▓▓▓▓ leaned into a razor-sharp wind and struggled through crusted snow in search of yellow patches that one day may allow scientists to predict nutritional problems in wildlife.

Caribou scramble to escape the helicopter ferrying ▓▓▓▓▓▓ and wildlife technician John ▓▓▓▓ onto the frozen tundra in this remote section of Denali National Park.

Casting this way and that, ▓▓▓▓▓ and ▓▓▓▓ checked urine-stained snow that may have been left by the fleeing animals.

I don't know how hungry *you* are, but when it comes to good eatin'...

Toilet-Seat Firms Sit Down and Talk

Two companies that believe there may be a lucrative market in sanitary toilet seats have reached an agreement in principle to merge.

Sheldon Fun Days includes nose picking contest

SHELDON — Sheldon children will finally be rewarded for breaking the rules Saturday — right on Main Street.

"You Can't Do That In Sheldon" activites at 4 p.m. Saturday are apart of Sheldon Fun Days which starts Friday. They include a nose picking contest, squirt-gun fights, water balloons, and other misbehavior.

From the "It tastes even better than yellow snow" department:

Candy consumers love the taste of Boogers

Stratford, Conn.
by the Associated Press

Tom Berquist was sitting at the dinner table with friends talking about why children like vulgar things, when he came up with an idea for a new candy.

He named it Boogers.

FREE

For Qualified Senior Citizens and Persons With Low Income

Spay/Neuter Service

This will cure Grandpa's friskiness...

Some Pieces of Rock Hudson Sold at Auction

Associated Press

New York

An auction of memorabilia and furnishings from actor Rock Hudson's Beverly Hills mansion brought in $216,452 yesterday, with fans bid-

Talk about owning a piece of the rock.

Airline personnel are quick to point out that flying is the safest way to travel. They'll give you persuasive statistics that compare the number of accidents to the number of miles traveled. Many go so far as to say that flying is safer than walking. Well, that may be true but when is the last time you saw an insurance machine in a shoe store? No thanks...

I'LL TAKE THE BUS

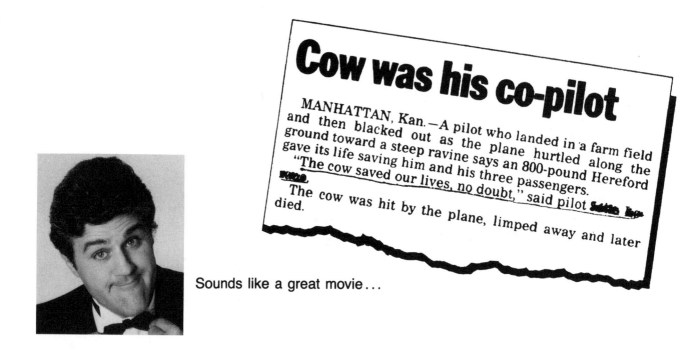

Cow was his co-pilot

MANHATTAN, Kan.—A pilot who landed in a farm field and then blacked out as the plane hurtled along the ground toward a steep ravine says an 800-pound Hereford gave its life saving him and his three passengers.

"The cow saved our lives, no doubt," said pilot ~~Mike Ing~~.

The cow was hit by the plane, limped away and later died.

Sounds like a great movie...

Pilot was wearing blinders

KINGSBURY, N.Y. — A student pilot wearing blinders was at the controls of a plane that collided with another aircraft over the Adirondacks, killing five people, authorities said Monday.

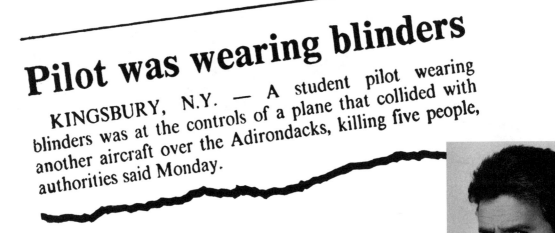

Blinders! I'd rather have the cow as my co-pilot than this guy.

Engine falls off plane, lands safely at O'Hare

CHICAGO (AP) — A Boeing 737 jetliner "lunged" and lurched after one of its engines fell off shortly after takeoff yesterday, but the pilot safely landed the plane, and none of the 32 people aboard were injured, officials said.

So if you want to be assured of landing safely, sit on the engine.

Council acts to ban airplanes on city streets

The Louisville City Council took the first step Tuesday evening to stop pilots from using land in the city as an airstrip without prior approval from the council.

It's about time. How many times have you pulled into a parking space only to see a DC-10 sitting there?

45

Pilot's injuries minor after crash

Associated Press

MANASSAS — Officials say a single-engine plane leaving Manassas Airport today crashed near the airport, but the pilot suffered only minor injuries.

A federal aviation spokeswoman said the crash could have been caused by the wings falling off the experimental plane. Kathleen Ber-

Hey, hey, hey, I wouldn't jump to any conclusions.

For many, sports headlines are among the most exciting in the newspaper, touting the record-breaking home run, the tie-breaking basket, the 90-yard run for the touchdown. Far more commonplace, though, are the foul balls that go into the stands and clunk the peanut vendor, in basketball the elbow in the eye, and in boxing the always humiliating, "He slipped in his own vomit." And so, here are the headlines that make up our sporting heritage...

THE SPORTING LIFE

Skiing season opens in Iran

When I think of a skiing vacation. I think of three places: Vail... Aspen... Tehran.

Death in the ring: Most boxers are not the same afterward

Yeah, I hear some of them are actually smarter.

Prior to the game, Larry Smith was placed on the injured list for the third time this season due to a <u>strained right thing</u>.

According to his wife, his left thing is still functioning perfectly.

Pool Tournament
Every Tuesday Evening
At
7:30 P.M.
Double Elimination
$2 Entry Fee

Grand Opening Postponed Until Further Notice

Where is it? No wonder it's postponed.

6th Annual Youth Fishing Derby Sept. 5

The 5th Annual youth fishing derby, sponsored by Fountainhead State Park, will be held Sept. 5 at Picken's Lake, Fountainhead State Park Area No. 3.

Registration will be from 8:30 to 9 a.m. and tournament fishing from 9 to 11:30 a.m. A picnic lunch will be at 12 noon.

Prizes will be awarded to three age divisions, 6-8, 9-11 ages of hotdog buns or one package of potato chips.

Entrants must bring their own bait and tackle. Youth must also be accompanied by parents or an adult guardian.

Participants must comply with all fishing regulations and must use a cane pole or rod and reel. **No dynamite or electrical devices will be permitted.**

Talk about taking all the fun out of fishing, huh.

50

Crappie Derby set for March

Better wear old clothes.

Most players on injured reserve apparently are actually injured

It kinda takes away your faith in the game, doesn't it?

51

Ski areas closed due to snow

Well, let's hope it warms up soon, eh.

Lack of water hurts ice fishing

The best ice fishing is oc
curring in backwaters char
nels that have enough wate
And there's not many i
northern Illinois.

Think how
the fish feel...

In today's modern society with Mom working, Dad putting in extra hours, and the kids involved in extracurricular activities, family time together becomes more important. But how should that time be spent? That's what we'll be looking at in...

FAMILY FUN

MULE DAY

*ENTERTAINMENT FOR THE
ENTIRE FAMILY*

• Syrup Making • Flea Market • Arts & Crafts • Cake Walk • Rooster Sailing • Pedal Power Tractor Pull for Children • Turkey Shoot with Sling Shot

You know, if we all thought for a minute, I think we could find a crueler way to torture that turkey.

And when the kids tire of that slingshot...

Saxon Arms

Badger™ *Great Family Indoor Fun!*

NEXT WEEKEND DO SOMETHING SPECIAL FOR DAD

Take him for free tea and cookies at the garbage incinerator.

Next weekend there is a public Open House at the Lower Mainland's new—and first—refuse incinerator in Burnaby. You'll get a look at the plant to see how it works, receive a pin and other free handouts. And there will be entertainment—the magic of Imagination Market, children's shows, Rikki Recycle and more—coffee, tea, milk, juice and cookies. Free.

You want some gravy on your Nuprin, Ma?

FATHER'S DAY SALE

Save 25-30%
All Lingerie

It's our semi-annual Foundation Sale! Stock up and save on our entire line of Bras, Briefs, Bikinis, Shapers and Daywear Coordinates for Women.

A. Reg. $16 **Sale $12.** Signature Collection underwire bra of nylon crepe. B, C cup.
B. Reg. $11 **Sale 8.25.** JCPenney seamless polyester contour bra.
C. Reg. $3 **Sale 2.44.** Tailored bikini of combed cotton. Sizes S, M, L. •
D. Reg. 2.75 **Sale 2.19.** Bright Vivana® nylon brief with cotton panel. Sizes S, M, L.

Shop our Fall Maternity Catalog for a great selection of comfortable fashions—from dresses to leisurewear.

LINE
CATALOG SHOPPING 1-800

For that
special dad
who likes to
dress up.

Did you ever read something and do a double take? You know you got it right the first time, but still, you go back and check anyway. Or to put it in layman's terms...

YOU WANNA RUN THAT BY ME AGAIN, PAL?

Ss. Peter and Paul to show pornography film

Ss. Peter and Paul Parish will sponsor a showing

I heard the church was getting more liberal, but this is ridiculous.

Wisconsin bill would permit blind to hunt deer

From News staff

A bill overwhelmingly passed by the Wisconsin state legislature would allow blind people to roam the woods to hunt deer — provided they are accompanied by a guide to help point their weapons.

It's about time! This bill has been bottled up in the legislature long enough.

The Good News Announcer

How lovely on the mountains are the feet of him who brings Good News, who Announces peace, And brings Good News of happiness. Who Announces salvation, And says to Zion, "Your God Reigns!" Isaiah 52:7

"FOR, BY, AND ABOUT SOUTH FLORIDA CHRISTIANS"

Vol . 5 No. 5	Thanksgiving/Christmas 1988	$1.00

"By this all men will know you are My disciples, If you have love for one another." - John 13:35

THE END IS HERE!

What's the bad news?

Man sues over mouse head in peanuts

Says he popped it in his mouth at an A's game; Coliseum is a defendant

Free mouse heads? Gee, when I was a kid all they had was Bat Day.

Eating dirt still a hard habit to break

LEXINGTON, Miss. — *(news)* Johnson tried hard to kick the habit. She took up smoking. She began eating laundry starch as a substitute. But the old craving still lingered.

I guess after a fast-food diet anything looks good.

Woman not injured by cookie

Staff Reporter

SARATOGA SPRINGS — A Saratoga Springs woman was not injured when she found a sewing needle in a Girl Scout cookie Thursday and wants to set the record straight.

Okay, she was lucky *this* time.

International Scientific Group Elects Bimbo As Its Chairman

Looks like Jessica Hahn may have a job after all.

Drought turns coyotes to watermelons

ATLANTA (AP) — Coyotes have a well-deserved reputation as chicken thieves, but in the dry year of 1988 they are also raiding south Georgia watermelon patches.

It's not the coyotes that bother me, it's those damn seeds.

Pants Man to expand at the rear

Maurice "The Pants Man," the large-volume discount clothing store, will expand its Millbury Street main store with a two-story addition in the rear. Construction of the addition, which will face Harding Street, began several weeks ago and is expected to be completed by the middle of April, according to ~~Mayor~~, a store official.

Stop eating that watermelon!

Furniture Drive for Homeless Launched

I'm sure that dinette set will look nice on Main Street, but shouldn't we be finding homes first?

Gerbil Selected Student Leader

NORWICH, England (AP) — A gerbil named Ken, campaigning on a platform of free beer and soft toilet paper, beat five other candidates to become president of the Student Union at the University of East Anglia.

It's amazing how the smartest ones always rise to the top.

FFA proposes name change to FFA

A proposed name change for the National Future Farmers of America organization has blessings from the current state FFA leaders, according to State FFA President Tim Teel.

The proposed amendment to the national constitution calls for the name to be changed from the National Future Farmers of America to the National FFA. It will be voted upon during the national convention, Nov. 10 to 12, in Municipal Auditorium, Kansas City, MO.

I guess the tough part is going to be changing all the stationery.

Dinosaur faces grand jury probe

Allegations of misconduct by public officials in the energy boomtown of Dinosaur are being investigated

The lawyer says his client will be extinct by the time the case comes to trial.

Searchers find Big Ugly child

BIG UGLY, W.Va. — A child, who spent 17 hours

Man shot, stabbed; death by natural causes ruled

Associated Press

ROCHESTER — ████████ County Medical Examiner Dr. ████████ ████ did not express shock or surprise that two of his investigators had ruled a 62-year-old man who was shot in the head and stabbed had died of natural causes.

"I don't think they were lackful, cavalier or something like that," ████████ said Tuesday. He called the mistake an "erroneous judgment."

Family catches fire just in time, chief says

The Richard Harder family Sunday returned home from church just in time, Lindsey Fire Chief Tom Overmyer said.

The family, of ~~3432 Sandusky~~ ~~Crosspointed ave~~, got back from church about 11:15 a.m. to find their kitchen table on fire and

Think of that. What are the odds on the whole family catching fire at the same time?

32 ignorant enough to serve on North jury

WASHINGTON — After four days of questioning prospective jurors, the judge and lawyers in Oliver North's Iran-Contra trial are learning that even in this news hub there are people who do not care about what is happening.

By the end of Friday's session, U.S. District Judge Gerhard A. Gesell declared 24 women and eight men ignorant enough of North's 1987

Here's a headline that pretty much says it all.

Braille dictionary for sale. Must see to appreciate!

Call Jerry

Think a lawyer
wrote this one?

CHARITY BAZAAR

SATURDAY & SUNDAY ONLY!

Support Our Salina Area Clubs
And Organizations

- Baked Goods
- Ticket Sales
- Craft Items
- And More!

AND

Don't Miss the United Way Celebration!

Activities and Demonstrations All Day
Saturday and Sunday — Including a Child Choking
Training Program Saturday at 2:00 p.m.

Come Join The Fun!

That pretty much takes care of your baby-sitting problem.

From the "We've got to destroy this village to save it" department:

City Increasing Speed Limit to Slow Down Drivers

The Powder Springs City Council Monday increased the speed limit on three city streets from 25 to 35 miles per hour, but delayed a decision on whether to raise the speed limit on Brownsville Road. Action on the

Organ expert impressed by ones here

By Staff Writer

When it comes to organs, we in Helena just don't know how good we've got it.

So it *is* size and not technique that counts.

• First Annual Animal Abuse Council Benefit Pig Roast, ███████. 9 a.m. trail ride (bring your own horse), 2 p.m. Pig Roast, Saturday, American Ozarks Campground, Highway 86 and JJ, Blue

---

Keep totally current with these titles in

Infectious Disease

You can try them FREE!

Swap 'em. Trade 'em with your friends. Collect the whole set.

CORRECTION
The China Seafood
Restaurant ad
that ran in last Tuesday's
Pennysaver/News
was incorrect.
It read
中國熊超茶室
It should have read
店效鮮海國中
We regret any
inconvenience this
may have caused.

I thought there was
something funny
the first time I saw that.

Ban On Nude Dancing On Governor's Desk

THE 1988 GEORGIA LEGISLATURE

ATLANTA (AP) — Gov. Joe Frank Harris' signature is the only step remaining to ban nude dancing in bars in Georgia.

Harris has said he would "look favorably" at the bill, which would take effect immediately upon his signature.

The idea's six-year journey through the Legislature ended Thursday when the Senate voted 44-7 to prohibit liquor license holders from offering live nude dancing or films depicting nudity or simulated sex acts.

The bill includes detailed definitions of impermissible nudity which apparently could not be

belt bill by next week.

—The Senate Education Committee approved a bill to require sex education in all public schools, but it added a provision allowing parents to remove their children from such classes.

But what you do in your house is your business.

Organ recital fades after firm beginning

Organist Frederick Swann made his name at posh churches of Chicago and Manhattan before heading west to Robert Schuller's Crystal Cathedral in Southern California, where he plays the organ and directs the music program.

Monday night, appearing in recital at Southwestern Baptist Theological Seminary in Fort Worth, he performed a program concentrating on romantic and mainstream 20th-century organ music.

Swann put his best foot forward first, with a radiant rendition of French com-

Tell me about it.

"I hope they found nothing wrong" department:

Building burns to the ground following safety inspection

Town of Pewaukee — A fire inspector was forced to flee a building he had just finished inspecting Thursday when the structure caught fire and burned to the ground.

Cows 'perform' to benefit ballet troupe

████████ gives puzzled look to Yuma ballerinas and their cow, which will do its 'dancing' Saturday

Okay, so it's not New York, but...

Everyone is familiar with Mark Twain's famous quote, "The reports of my death have been greatly exaggerated." It just goes to show, the more things change, the more they remain the same. That's why we've entitled this chapter:

SORRY, OUR RECORDS SHOW YOU'RE DEAD

Tax return may be required after death

May be required? Could I find out now so I can rest in peace?

Ohio man, 79, pronounced dead, but says he feels much better now

Man's 'serious' condition an improvement over death

Associated Press

KNOXVILLE — ~~Bklwkhp Bhmw sb Bhmw~~ was listed in serious condition Sunday at Park West Hospital — but he's in better shape than earlier when he was declared dead.

Wait till he gets the bill. He might change his mind.

It's official: Dead people can't vote

AUGUSTA — After 22 years answering last-minute election questions from city and town clerks, ███████████ didn't bat an eye Monday when a caller asked her if the dead can vote.

"Some lady voted absentee Saturday and died Sunday," ███████ explained later as she recalled the query. "Can they count the ballot?"

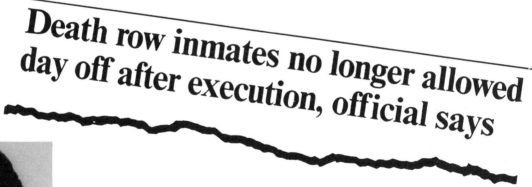

I guess this reporter never lived in Chicago.

Death row inmates no longer allowed day off after execution, official says

Boy, you thought the other warden was tough.

81

Woman dead when head removed

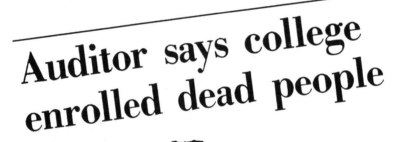

Auditor says college enrolled dead people

— (UPI) — ▮▮▮▮ Junior College officials may have registered dead students and misclassified hundreds of nursing home residents to increase registration figures and obtain more state money, a preliminary audit says.

I think I was in some of those classes.

'Butcher of Balkans' dies

BELGRADE, Yugoslavia—Andrija Artukovic, who was extradited from the United States and convicted of ordering thousands of prisoners killed in World War II, has died in jail at the age of 88.

Known as the "Butcher of the Balkans," Artukovic had been sentenced to death by firing squad in May 1986, but his execution had ← been postponed indefinitely because of his ill health.

Death may ease tension

PORT-AU-PRINCE, Haiti (UPI) — Diplomats say the death of Col. Jean-Claude Paul, a suspected drug trafficker who died after eating what police believe was poisoned pumpkin soup, may help ease tensions between the United States and Haiti.

Yeah, but what if it doesn't!

UWM theater training dead for '88

I guess they must need more help at the Motor Vehicles Bureau.

Receiving a cremated relative in the mail can be a rude shock

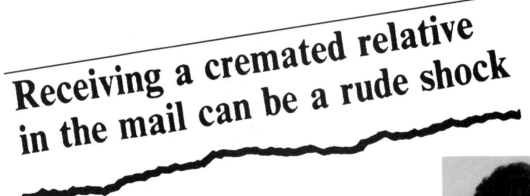

Hey, Ma, Grandpa's back!

Funny, WM seeks enthusiastic aud. for headline bk. Must enjoy reading about plane crashes, condoms, and people who aren't really dead. No weirdos, please.

SPEAKING PERSONALLY

Oh why did you have to die and leave this Earth so early? Every day I grieve that you are no longer with us. This message dedicated to my wife's first husband.

M.H.L.

MERV'S MOWERS

Merv. is out of jail now & back at his shop in ▬▬▬▬. He welcomes all of his old customers. For honest mower repairs, call

The cops never would have caught him if his riding lawn mower hadn't stalled outside the bank.

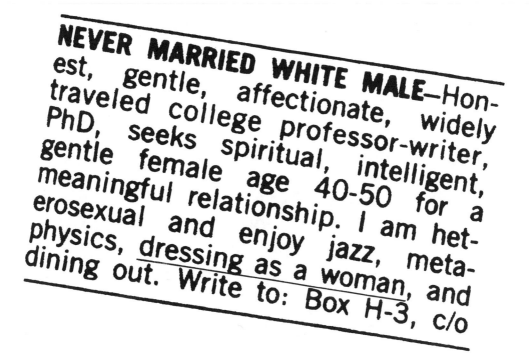

NEVER MARRIED WHITE MALE—Honest, gentle, affectionate, widely traveled college professor-writer, PhD, seeks spiritual, intelligent, gentle female age 40-50 for a meaningful relationship. I am heterosexual and enjoy jazz, metaphysics, <u>dressing as a woman</u>, and dining out. Write to: Box H-3, c/o

Jazz? Who likes jazz?

"Ads that speak for themselves" department:

MUST SELL: Health food store, due to failing health.   1-8

"Do you think this guy watches Donahue?" department:

FARMER LOOKING FOR WIFE WITH TRACTOR
If interested, please send picture of tractor: P. O. Box 2518,

"You show me yours, I'll show mine" department:

NOTICE TO ANYONE wishing to go to Van Wert, Dec. 12, for hernia opera-tion, contact ~~March 1~~

LOST DONALD DUCK WALLET - Need for identification. Please call. ~~xxxxxxx~~.

If you find it, please call Vice President Dan Quayle immediately.

Will swap **white satin wedding gown** (worn once) for 50 pounds fresh **Gravy Train.**

Sure, she's got a big appetite but she's cheap to feed.

MOVING SALE - Wheelchair, hospital bed, deluxe sliding chair stair glide, and a motorcycle.

Gosh, I wonder what happened.

Young man, 20, wants job on stud farm w/rm., prefer to work for a lady. ~~████████~~, Box 87134, **College Park** 30337. ~~████████~~ aft. 6 p.m.

Nice work if you can get it.

"Boy, kids grow up fast today" department:

Babysitter - Looking for infant to babysit in my home. Excellent references.

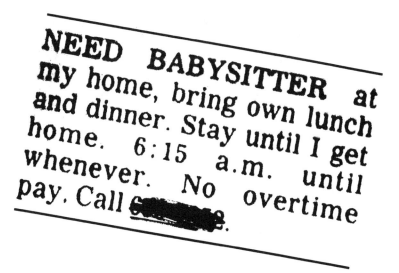

NEED BABYSITTER at my home, bring own lunch and dinner. Stay until I get home. 6:15 a.m. until whenever. No overtime pay. Call ~~████████~~.

Ask for Ebeneazar.

510   Help Wanted

VACANCY for a part-time Breastfeeding Coordinator. 20 hours/week, $6.50/hour. Looking for organized person with public relation, teaching and record-keeping skills. Breastfeeding Experience preferred, but not required.

Coordinator? You're pretty much limited to two choices, aren't you?

NEED Plain Clothes Security. Must have shop lifting experience. Apply between 8a.m.-3p.m. Mon.-Fri., at ▬▬▬▬▬, suite 207.

Hmmm...murder, burglary, assault...Sorry, we're looking for someone with shoplifting experience.

600-General

AIR TRAFFIC CONTROL. FAA accepting applications now. $24,000-$62,000. No aviation experience necessary. All day exam preparation course.

At least at the other job you had to have some shoplifting experience.

SURGICAL ASSISTANT

NO EXP NEC. Execl career opp'ty for a bright, dependable person who likes people. We will train you in our busy Mt Kisco Oral surgery office. Salary & benefits open

I hear this is the job you get if you're turned down as a security guard or air traffic controller.

Town of South Hadley: An equal opportunity employer. Reliable person needed to remove dead animals on public roadways. Persons interested contact South Hadley Board of Health at ████-████.

Gee, a once in a lifetime opportunity to enter the high-paying world of carcas removal.

Gorbachev launching glasnost? Oprah losing 67 pounds?
Pee Wee Herman a movie star?

WHO WOULDA THOUGHT?

Iran severs relations with Iran

Even *they* don't like themselves!

"Apply now" department:

In the sewers, each day's job has new allure

Charcoal briquettes destroyed by fire

Associated Press

ELK GROVE, Calif. — Fire broke out in a warehouse containing more than 1,000 tons of charcoal briquettes, authorities said.

It had to be arson. Do you know how hard it is to light those stupid briquettes?

Advertising is big business in this country. Companies spend a fortune doing market research, demographic surveys, psychological profiles—all in an effort to make their product seem different from the competition's. Well, the products you'll see in this next group of advertisements certainly are. That's why we call this chapter:

YOU'RE SELLING WHAT?

Flu doesn't take a holiday, and neither do we!

At Memorial Community Hospital we realize that you can get sick at any time. That's why we offer convenient medical care at both Health Branch West and at our Emergency Trauma Center throughout the year.

Our Emergency Trauma Center is open 365 days a year, **24 hours a day,** so you can get medical care when you need it throughout the holidays.

Health Branch West Holiday Hours

behind Hy-Vee, next to Capital Mall

9 a.m.-7 p.m.
Monday-Saturday

Noon-6 p.m.
Sunday

CLOSED THANKSGIVING DAY

No Appointment Necessary

Professional and personal care
where you live and work.

MEMORIAL COMMUNITY HOSPITAL

Better not choke
on that turkey...

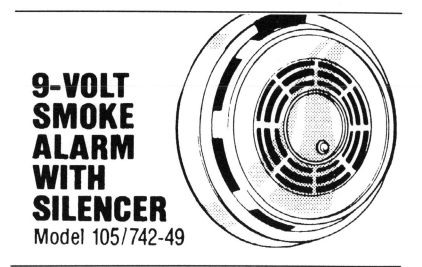

9-VOLT SMOKE ALARM WITH SILENCER
Model 105/742-49

Yeah, the last thing you need is this thing waking you up in the middle of the night, huh?

"Ollie North shuffle" department:

You can learn to dance like a Contra

This is the first time a class for learning contras has been offered at Leisure World. What is a contra? A contra is almost literally a dance of opposition. It is usually performed by many couples, face to face, line facing line, in long lines normally formed lengthwise of the hall, so that the head of the line is at the caller's end of the hall. It is becom-

PICTORIAL DENTURE

(A COMBINATION OF DENTAL TECHNOLOGY AND PHOTOGRAPHIC ART)

This invention has been developed for identification and transformation of the tiresome task of constructing dentures into a pleasant artistic process.

The upper denture contains a transparent color picture which will remain intact for the life of the denture.

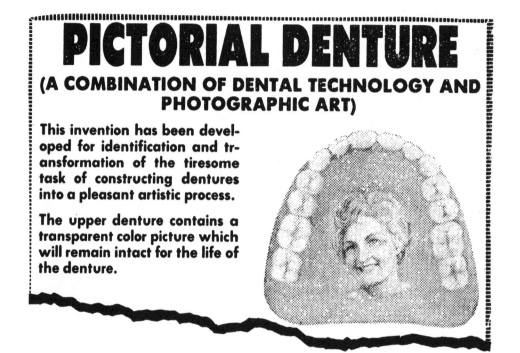

Be thankful these people are doing dental work and not proctology!

HONEYBAKED BRAND HAM

O.J.'S FAVORITE HOLIDAY MEAL

O.J., that's not a ham, it's a turkey.
If anyone should know a pigskin, it should be O.J.

"Hey, this dog is dented" department:

McComb Supply's Annual
CAT & DOG SALE!
SCRATCHED & DENTED ITEMS

SALE STARTS
MARCH 2nd & 3rd
Thurs. & Fri.
From
7:30 A.M.
TO
4:30 P.M.

ALL FLOOR SAMPLES
10% OFF
(EXCEPT APPLIANCES & T.V.s)

REGISTERED MINIATURE American Eskimos, females-$150, male-$125. Ready to go.

Buy two. Keep them in the freezer.

"Eat quick before it escapes" department:

103

Harper's Boneless Old-Fashioned Pit Barbeque. Old fashioned microwaveable package. Warm up for a delicious . Sandwich in a minute
#711 . . 2 to 3 lbs. avg. $12.25

Old-fashioned microwave? Remember Grandma's day when it took up to *three* minutes to microwave a package?

"If rabbit feet were lucky, they'd still be on the rabbit" department:

RABBIT fur coat, size medium $45. Small hutch, $55.

#T1758 WINDPROOF PANEL BRIEF $15.50
(Please specify size)

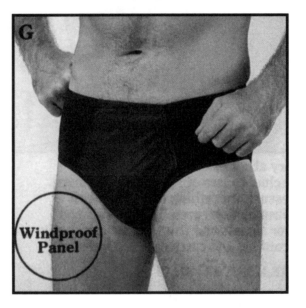

Windproof
Panel

Windproof? If it wasn't for the wind,
this guy wouldn't get any action at all.

Kids Are Grreat Meals

Packed in novelty cartons with surprise. All meals include beverage.

Buy One
And Get One FREE!

with this coupon
Good Through 2/29/88

People who eat kids? What's that? A Geraldo show?

MUST SELL!
3 grave spaces in Laureland, very reasonable. Plus air-conditioner.

If you get the plot next to the air conditioner, it would be a good place to use the windproof underwear.

This last chapter is one of my favorites. I can understand how, under the pressure of deadlines, a misplaced word or ungrammatical sentence can slip by, but when a picture is placed next to a headline, you assume the two are related and when you find out they're not, well, it makes you wonder. Impossible, you say? How could that happen?

PICTURE THIS

Living

Manuel Dias, The Modesto Bee

One body in yard identified

SACRAMENTO, Calif. (AP) — One of the seven bodies found buried outside a boardinghouse was identified as that of an alcoholic who spent most of his life on the streets, but authorities don't know how he or the others died.

The body of Benjamin Fink, 60, a former resident of Dorothea Puente's boardinghouse in downtown Sacramento, was identified Monday through

Dirty job

President and Mrs. Reagan shovel dirt at the groundbreaking ceremony for the Reagan Presidential Library in Simi Valley, Calif., Monday.

**"Call for backup. I don't know
how many of them are in there"
department:**

Drugs seized from cyclists

The Daily Times

Parading — The Preschoolers of
First United Methodist Church held a
bicycle and tricycle parade in the
parking lot behind the school Friday
afternoon.

The Arizona Republic, Doyle Sanders

DEADLY CAST / State Game and Fish Department personnel spray rotenone, a poison that kills only fish and some aquatic insects, into a Lake Pleasant cove. The department earlier this week said <u>killing all the fish in three coves is the most accurate method of determining the lake's fish population.</u> They added that the poison poses no danger to swimmers or water skiers.

Now, if they don't kill every fish, will it still be accurate?

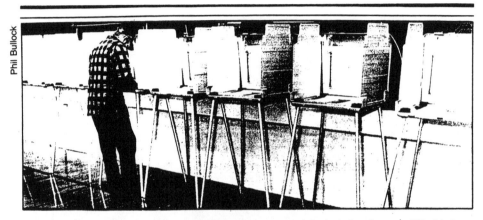

Voters trickled to the polls early this morning, including this solitary voter who cast his ballot shortly after polls opened at Willow School.

Local voting heaviest in years

Looks like it's going to be a close race.

"Has Jimmy Swaggart heard about this?" department:

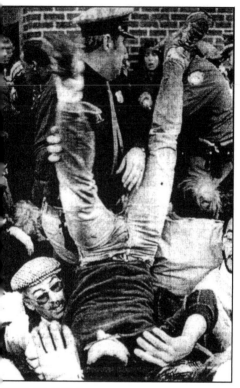

AP/Wide World Photos

Seduction costly for ex-pastor

Associated Press

TACOMA, Wash. — A woman who sued her former pastor for seducing her has been awarded $130,000 by a jury, a verdict intended partly as a warning to other ministers.

"We want the community to see that this can't keep happening," juror Cathy Zurfluh said Friday. "It's got to stop somewhere."

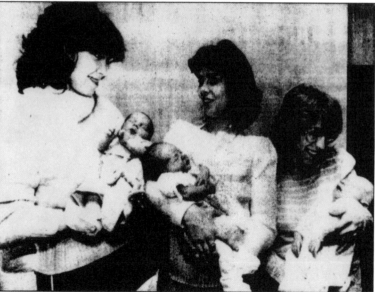

Baby cousins

These Chattanooga-area sisters all had babies a day apart to finish out 1986. From left are ████ with son, ████, born on Dec. 29; ████ with son, ████, born Dec. 31; and ████ with daughter, ████, born Dec. 30. (AP Photo)

Does Steve Garvey know about this?

Former affair's result has grown too big for this couple to ignore

113

U.S. troops going to Honduras

WASHINGTON (AP) — About 3,200 American infantry and airborne troops are flying to Honduras today in the most dramatic show of U.S. force in the six-year Nicaraguan war, causing the Senate's top Democrat to accuse President Reagan of "overreaction."

The White House described the movement as "an emergency deployment readiness exercise" triggered by what it called the invasion of Honduras by 1,500 to 2,000 Nicaraguan forces pursuing Contra rebels.

The exercise involves two battalions of the 82nd Airborne Division from Fort Bragg, N.C., and two battalions from the 7th Infantry Division at Fort Ord, Calif.

The troops will be posted out of harm's way for an indefinite period near the Palmerola Air Force Base in Honduras, about 125 miles from the area of reported hostilities, said Marlin Fitzwater, the president's spokesman.

"This exercise is a measured response designed to show our staunch support to the democratic government of Honduras at a time when its territorial integrity is being violated by the Cuban- and Soviet-supported Sandinista army," Fitzwater said in a late-night announcement.

He said it also was "a signal to the governments and peoples of Central America of the seriousness with which

the United States government views the current situation in the region."

Some congressional Democrats weren't buying the administration's rationale.

"It's an overreaction," said Senate Majority Leader Robert Byrd, D-W.Va. "The Sandinistas have crossed over the border before and gone back."

"I just hope it's merited," Sen. John Kerry, D-Mass., said, recalling a similar incident two years ago when the United States jumped to the aid of Honduras under circumstances many saw as exaggerated by the White

(See TROOPS, page 12)

Monroe Evening Times

Juveniles recaptured in Bacliff

BACLIFF — Two juveniles who escaped from a youth group home in Galveston Thursday and threatened to shoot a police officer were apprehended around 6 p.m. that day, according to a Galveston County Sheriff's Department spokeswoman.

Reports show the two youths and a companion escaped from the home sometime Thursday morning and were discovered inside a Bacliff residence around noon by a police officer. The spokeswoman said she did not know which law enforcement department the officer was from.

The officer left the house to wait for assistance after the juveniles raised a shotgun and threatened to kill him, the spokeswoman said. By the time the backup officers arrived, the juveniles had left the home.

One of the youths was captured a short time later about two blocks from the house. The other two led officers on a five-hour chase in which a DPS helicopter and several other vehicles were utilized, reports indicate.

The youths were apprehended around 6 p.m. at the end of 16th Street.

All three juveniles were charged

SEE JUVENILES, PAGE 2

HARE-RAISING VISIT — Thomas Phillips, 9 months, and Sharell Phillips, 2, of Allentown, Pa., didn't much enjoy their visit with the Easter Bunny at a mall Friday.

If you want to catch
a criminal, you have
to think like
a criminal...

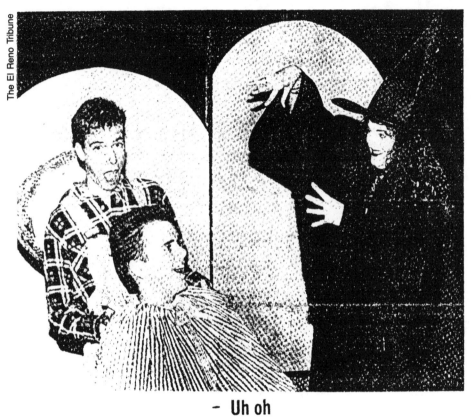

Moslem extremists renew threats against hostages

BEIRUT, Lebanon (AP) — Shiite Moslem extremists holding U.S. hostages repeated their long-standing demands for the Americans' release in a new statement, threatening reprisal if the demands are not met.

- Uh oh

Americans are eating way to grave

WASHINGTON (AP) — Millions of Americans are waddling their way to early graves by consuming too much fat, too much salt and washing it all down with too much booze, the U.S. surgeon general reported on Wednesday.

"Diseases of dietary excess and imbalance" are among the leading causes of death in the United States, said the report issued by C. Everett Koop. "Over-consumption ... is now a major concern for Americans."

The study said that of 2.1 million Americans who died last year, nearly 1.5 million succumbed to diseases associated with diet.

"What we eat may affect our risk for several of the leading causes of death for Americans, notably coronary heart disease, stroke, atherosclerosis, diabetes, and some types of cancer," the report said. "These disorders together now account for more than two-thirds of all deaths in the United States."

The study said that many Americans are too fat, while others fail to get required nutrients such as calcium and iron. And the report repeatedly emphasized the need to cut down on consumption of animal products and replace them with a greater variety of foods, particularly fruits, vegetables and whole grains.

Nutrition experts praised the report, predicting that may have an important impact on how Americans regard their diet and on products sold by the food industry.

Charles J. Carey, president of the National Food Processors Association, said the report will encourage companies to develop products that follow the guidelines endorsed in the report.

Though the report acknowledges that malnutrition remains a problem in some parts of the world and for certain Americans, it says that "for most of us the more likely problem has become one of overeating — too many calories for our activity levels and an imbalance in the nutrients

Bedford Gazette

"If you miss class, we'll hold you under" department:

A police officer and a resident wade through floodwaters in the town of Uribia on Wednesday after Hurricane Joan hit the Colombian coast.

Classes to help public spot 'fishy' seafood

Staff Writer

TALLAHASSEE — Declaring that "the best inspectors in the world are an educated public," members of Florida's fishing industry on Wednesday announced a series of seminars aimed at teaching consumers how to spot problem seafood.

The fish dealers and industry lobbyists staged a news conference to announce that they hope to ease public concerns over recent outbreaks of seafood-related illnesses and revelations of fish fraud, including the deliberate substitution of inexpensive fillets for popular catches such as grouper and red snapper.

"The seafood business, just like any other business, has its good and its bad," said Mike Abrams, owner of Captain Mike's seafood stores in Hallandale and Fort Lauderdale. "We think the good far outweighs the bad."

Standing before an elaborate display of fresh seafood, Robert Jones, executive director of the Tallahassee-based Southeastern Fisheries Association, said: "These are legitimate and bona fide fishermen who see their businesses diminishing. They feel there is another side to the story."

Jones said the majority of fishermen

SEE **FISH** / 15A

"I feel like I'm wearing nothing at all" department:

AP/Wide World Photos

New devices jolt, restart hearts of cardiac victims

The Associated Press

BOSTON — New devices that automatically deliver heart-starting electrical jolts and can be operated with little training could save many of the 400,000 Americans who die each year of cardiac arrest, according to a new report.

The Topeka Capital-Journal

Heading for national

The Jefferson County 4-H meat judging team, winners in the Kansas state contest Aug. 27 in Emporia, practiced in a Topeka grocery this past week for the

▩▩▩▩▩▩▩▩▩▩, Valley Falls veterinariar
Team members are, from left, ▩▩▩▩▩▩▩
▩▩▩▩▩▩▩▩▩▩▩▩▩▩▩▩▩▩▩▩▩▩

No comment.

Brad Hohenstreet photo

Quality time

~~Mary and Bill Hohenstreet~~ enjoy the shade of the trees — and the company of their grandson, ~~Phillip Butler~~, 6 — at Fenton City Park recently.

Some kids *demand* quality time and get it.

"Lock up your daughters"
 department:

John J. Watkins

WEENIE WAGON: A peculiar sight rolled down Cine Ave. in Griffith Tuesday. It was none other than the Oscar Mayer Wiener Mobile stopping to get gassed up at a local gas station.

Sex education requires parents

He dreams of Mars visi

EXCELLENT OUTLOOK — After receiving a broken neck in an accident, John Peck, staying at the Prescott Veterans Administration Medical Center, was tired of all the sad and sympathetic looks he was getting from passers-by. Peck decided to put the American flags on to his neck brace and now he says " people smile when they walk by."

Many years ago, when he was just eight, Brian O'Leary conceived his dream: "Let's go to Mars."

It's 1988, much time has passed and O'Leary has gone through some of life's passages, but his vision is still intact...only now greatly expanded. He wants the United States to join with Russia in a 1999 mission to Mars to herald in the millenium as an affirmation of world peace and unity.

To do this, he would scrap the Star Wars program, "a system that will not work," and put that money and work force toward going to the Red Planet and into other programs that would enrich the human condition.

The former astronaut, educator

You know, I think he'll make it.

'AA examining airlines' mechanical problems

ETROIT — The Federal Avia-Administration has quietly be-its first system-wide look at mechanical problems of air-es in daily service, according to ral officials.

cut back on the margin of safety by letting items go unrepaired for days at a time.

They say the airline industry's deregulation and intense competition has spurred cost-cutting carriers to put off repairs, trim maintenance facilities and lower their spare parts inventories.

The FAA's probe of a dozen of the nation's major airlines, which began on Aug. 10, is expected to last several months. Agency officials here and at other FAA facilities in Washington and across the country said the survey was not triggered by any specific complaint or event.

Air Line Pilots Association with prompting the federal action.

They also note that T. Allan McArtor, who became the FAA's administrator in July, has spoken of the MELS at recent meetings with aviation groups, indicating a concern about their impact on airplane safety.

AP/Wide World Photos

Takeoff position

~~████████~~, 7, is stretched out in flying form as he tries out his skateboard on a newly paved parking lot in downtown Adrian, Mich.

Looks a little tail heavy to me.

PROHIBITED
PEDESTRIANS
BICYCLES
MOTOR SCOOTERS
METAL TREADS
FARM IMPLEMENTS
ANIMALS ON FOOT

MORE HEADLINES

COMPILED BY JAY LENO

WITH PHOTOGRAPHS BY JOSEPH DEL VALLE
AND CARTOONS BY JACK DAVIS

ACKNOWLEDGMENTS

I would like to thank the following comedians and comedy writers for all their help and assistance:

Jimmy Brogan, Steve Crantz, Jim Edwards, Jon Kleinman, Wayne Kline, Joe Medeiros, Ron Richards, Kevin Rooney, Marvin Silbermintz and Buddy Winston.

Also, Robert Jarrin for opening all the envelopes.

My editor, Rick Horgan, for taking my dresser drawer full of headlines and putting them in order.

And my wife, Mavis, for having to listen to me constantly ask, "Honey, is this funny?"

Jay Leno
Los Angeles, California
June 15, 1990

CRIMESTOPPERS

Men in blue, the city's finest, society's protectors. These are just a few of the names used to describe today's law enforcement officers—a hardy breed who take no guff, call 'em as they see 'em, and give as good as they get. The headlines you're about to see show why we can all walk the streets without fear, confident they're on the job.

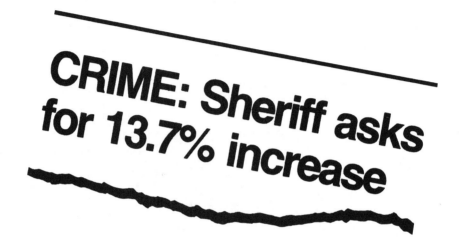

CRIME: Sheriff asks for 13.7% increase

Okay, Spike, you've been hitting two houses a week. Let's make that three. And Lefty, I want to see twice as many purse snatchings. Let's all do what we can to help the sheriff.

From the "Your tax dollars at work" department:

Sex fund pledged for sheriff

County officials have pledged **funds** for sheriff's officers to buy sex at massage parlors in order to run several remaining sexually oriented **businesses** out of Bexar County.

Hey, why should senators and congressmen have all the fun?

Outlaw to announce 3 police promotions

Hey, you don't think these guys are working together, do you?

Mayor says D.C. is safe except for murders

Oh, that's a relief. I was afraid I'd get my car radio stolen.

High-crime areas said to be safer

Now, if we could just increase crime in the low-crime areas, they'd be safer, too.

Slow Driver Arrested After 4-County Chase

Los Angeles

The California Highway Patrol booked a motorist for evading arrest and other charges after a long chase through four counties that never exceeded the speed limit, a spokesman said yesterday.

It's a good thing he wasn't parked.
It could've taken all day.

Police blotter

■ Sent city police out at 11:38 a.m. to kick kids off the roof of a downtown furniture store.

Farthest kick gets free donuts.

No cause of death determined for beheading victim

How about stretched vocal cords?

Jury suspects foul play in Chapman death

The 27-year-old Chapman apparently died as a result of a gunshot wound to the head. His body was then burned and buried in a shallow grave, the jury ruled.

We can't rule out the possibility of suicide.

Terrorist bought bomb parts at K mart

Attention K mart shoppers: plutonium on aisle 9...

Thieves steal burglar alarm

I wonder what they did with the Porsche that was attached to it.

Court rules that being a jerk is not a crime

ATLANTA (AP) — There's no law against being a jerk, a court has determined.

The Georgia Court of Appeals ruled that a former bank manager had no grounds to collect damages from her boss or an allegedly obnoxious co-worker, even if the co-worker was the boorish, obnoxious prankster that she claimed he was.

I guess we can all breathe easier tonight.

Would-be robber enters wrong door

CEREDO, W.Va. — An attempt to rob the state liquor store in the Ceredo Plaza shopping center this morning ended when the gunman realized he had walked into the YMCA branch instead, police said.

And yesterday he got mugged!

Robbery Suspect Mugged

A man stole $2,100 from a Brooklyn savings bank on Friday but was mugged as he made his getaway, so he immediately reported the crime to the nearest police station house, the police said. Officers promptly arrested the man.

You don't think this is the same guy who stole that burglar alarm, do you?

$3-million thief not greedy: Judge

Who says politicians and crooks think alike?

Ow! My hair's caught.... Ow!

Wanted: A hangman who knows the ropes

Prison spokesman Richard Bauer says they really need someone who knows the ropes, because precision is essential. Otherwise, the prisoner could get hurt during the procedure.

Robber's description: Man, possibly a woman, definitely ugly

Hmmm, the problem is going to be interviewing suspects without hurting their feelings.

Son mistakes mom for bird, shoots her

A 50-year-old Roanoke woman was shot Friday in Bedford County by her son, who said he mistook her for a turkey.

Hey, these giblets don't taste right...

Woman Who Ran Over Spouse Gets 5-15 Years

Told doctors he was possessed by Mickey Mouse

What a shame... and on his fiftieth anniversary, too.

"Hey, I thought we were just going for a walk" department:

Man charged with allegedly sexually assaulting pit bull

Resort cabbie accused of punching 101-year-old man; may lose license

Combined with that pit bull incident, he *should* lose his license.

Capt. Pizza robbed last week; $1100 and cheese taken

On Monday, August 8, at approximately 6 a.m., the owner of Captain Pizza on Cambridge Street informed police that a window and the front door of the restaurant had been smashed and an unknown person or persons had stolen $1100 and three blocks of cheddar cheese, valued at $240.

Did you ever think you'd see the day when someone could take the cheese from Captain Pizza?

Man charged with theft after attacking pizza

A 24-year-old Milton man has been charged with theft under $1,000 because he smashed a pizza to the ground.

Police say the man approached a woman who was carrying a take-out pizza at the corner of Prince and Pearl streets. He then allegedly grabbed the pizza box from her hands, threw it on the ground and stepped on it. Although the woman resisted, it was to no avail.

Looks like they're out to get the captain.

"Slightly damaged goods: half price off!" department:

A drunken-driving charge was filed against James ~~~~~ ~~~~~ after he urinated on 11 boxes of spaghetti in a 7-Eleven store last Thursday and then drove away.

"Hey this spaghetti tastes funny" department:

Police report in the Contra Costa Sun: "Police were called to an Orinda home after a 23-year-old woman became irate with her parents' nagging and threw spaghetti at her father. Neither parents nor the daughter wished prosecution, and all promised to contact their respective therapists."

Murder Charge Filed In Deadly Food Fight

A man, 18, was charged Tuesday with murdering his friend because the friend had thrown three hot dogs on their floor during a game, police said.

Imagine, if the man had ordered only two hot dogs, he might still be alive today.

"Hey, I said I was sorry" department:

Campus killer to remain in prison despite apology

"Don't fool with the Amish" department:

Dismembered victim not a pleasant fellow

A 22-year-old Pittsburgh man who was dismembered and his body parts scattered around Allegheny County was a nice guy with a bad attitude, according to his criminal record and some who knew him.

"He had a snippy attitude," said ~~Anthony Michalowski's~~ former stepfather, ~~Walter Engel of Pitts-burgh.~~ "I told him, 'You're going to get your throat cut someday.'"

Neighbors Say Sniper Not Very Neighborly

He was a quiet man, kind of a loner...

"Ridicule drove him to crime" department:

At 6:45 a.m., the House of Erotica bookstore at 102 E. Charleston Blvd., was the target of an attempted holdup by a masked gunman. A silent alarm, however, tipped off police who arrived on the scene in time to apprehend the bandit still inside.

He was identified as Gene Wayne Vagina, 20, of ████ Wyandotte St.

He's been teased his whole life, Your Honor...

Police recover stolen hamster, arrest 3

When burglars struck Immaculate Conception School in Bloomfield, their choice of loot quickly clued city police that the burglars weren't exactly big-time thieves.

Bypassing radios, typewriters and other valuable equipment, the burglars who struck May 7 at the school on Edmond Street made off with "Biddles," the pet hamster from the science classroom, and an aquarium containing two goldfish from the school secretary's desk.

Dog that bit 2 people ordered to leave town

The fate of Kirby, a Des Plaines dog accused of vicious behavior, could have been worse.

Cook County Circuit Judge Charles Loverde ruled Wednesday that Kirby must be sent out of Des Plaines, never to return.

How was this explained to the dog exactly?

From the "Winner of the sack race" department:

One-legged man competent to stand trial

LAWRENCE — The drifter who allegedly beat an elderly man with a hammer last month was found competent to stand trial yesterday after a 20-day evaluation at Bridgewater State Hospital.

147

Man says body is his wife, but she tells police it isn't

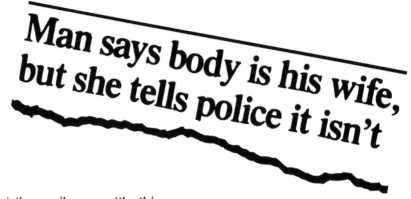

Let's let the mailman settle this.

Man, shot twice in head, gets mad!

Don't you hate people
who lose their temper?

SEEK AND YE SHALL FIND

Theologians tell us to find religion in our daily lives. Well, what better place to look for it than in our daily newspaper. Take these headlines, for example...

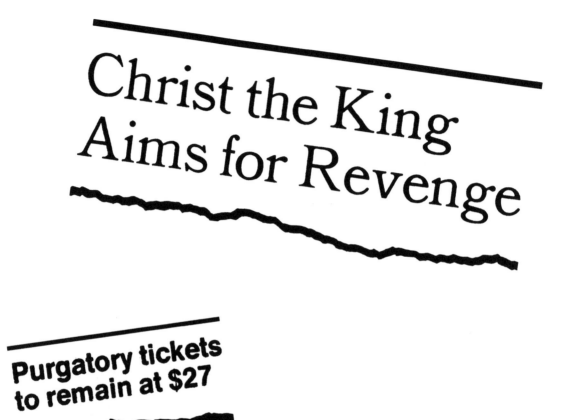

Christ the King Aims for Revenge

Purgatory tickets to remain at $27

Gee, I wonder if they give special rates for politicians and televangelists?

Sheriff and God Collide At Church Intersection

Tell that to your insurance company.

Christ to serve as presiding judge

I guess that pretty much rules out an appeal.

Pope to be arraigned for allegedly burglarizing clinic

Gee, donations must *really* be down this year.

THAT CAN'T BE RIGHT

This chapter contains headlines so ridiculous, so stupid, that we feel compelled to reiterate that they were actually taken from legitimate, non-tabloid newspapers. Is "serious journalism" a thing of the past? You be the judge...

Londoner fatally injured by turnip

LONDON: Police are investigating the death of a man who was fatally injured after being hit by a turnip thrown from a passing car. The attack apparently was carried out by a gang who toss vegetables at random at passers-by. "It sounds very amusing but clearly it is not because a man has died," a police official said.

When turnips are outlawed, only outlaws will have turnips.

140 miles of sewers taped for television viewing

Gee, don't you think network television is starting to get a little desperate?

Bland Music Competition Scheduled

Hey, is this how Zamphir, master of the pan flute, got started?

"Come to think of it, the *kids* don't say too much either—they just stay in their room all day" department:

Freeze-dried dog furnishes the fireplace

MEDINA, Wash. (AP) — Unlike most dogs, Puli the Hungarian sheepdog doesn't play on the furniture. Puli is the furniture.

Puli died in 1984, but his owners, Suzanne and Rob ▮▮▮▮▮, couldn't bear to part with the pooch that had been so much a part of their household in this affluent suburb east of Seattle.

So they had him freeze-dried.

Blind workers eye better wages

Is this the most sensitive way they could phrase this?

Uranium 'theme park' proposed at Oak Ridge

Gee, I wonder if it will glow in the dark?

"Four days, three nights in beautiful downtown Chernobyl" department:

Area man wins award for nuclear plant accident

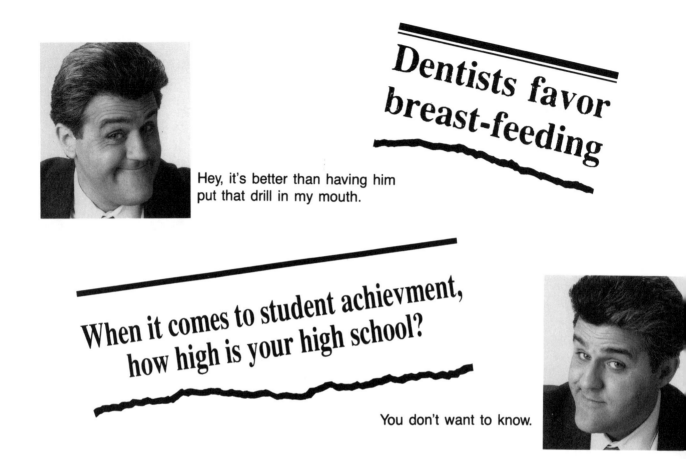

Dentists favor breast-feeding

Hey, it's better than having him
put that drill in my mouth.

When it comes to student achievment, how high is your high school?

You don't want to know.

"Gee, it's hard to believe the Japanese are ahead of us" department:

Schooling free but no room for students

Postal Service seeking ways to deliver mail more slowly

Has this been a problem?
People getting their mail too quickly?

Overnight, second-day mail will be delivered a day later

No comment.

"If you need any more proof that the Soviet threat is over" department:

Soviet 'biological weapon' was really bee poop

LOS ANGELES (AP) — The need to keep their offspring cool prompts Asian bees to produce "yellow rain" — excrement the U.S. government once believed was a Soviet biological weapon, researchers reported today.

From the "Old movie" department:

Helicopter powered by human flies

Human flies look like regular flies, except they say (in a little voice), "Help me...help me."

Car haunts owner from grave

MIAMI — Elio Mas, boss of the grave diggers at Flagler Memorial Park, told police someone stole his car, an '86 Mitsubishi Mirage.

Miami police found it for him. In a grave. In the cemetery where Mas works.

Shortly after 8:30 a.m., Wednesday, Feb. 22, 1989, a Sikorsky S76A Helicopter, leased by ~~Consolidated Co.~~ <u>made an unscheduled crash</u> a few yards off Rt. 19 at the Mansfield Rd. intersection in North Strabane Twp. Early speculation as to the probably cause of the crash was weather related.

Stick to the schedule. You're not supposed to crash until 9:00 P.M.

Surprise open house planned for Hillocks

Mr. and Mrs. Richard Hillock of Nevada will be honored at a surprise open house Sunday from 2 to 4 p.m. at Nevada Assembly of God Church,

Three ambulances take blast victim to hospital

Sorry about your torso, but the second ambulance got stuck in traffic...

TO SEAL - MOISTEN FLAP AND FOLD OVER.

DO NOT FOLD

STATE OF NEW JERSEY
DIVISION OF TAXATION
CN 274
TRENTON, NEW JERSEY 08646-0274

No comment.

A HOUSE IS NOT A HOME

Who among us is not touched by the plight of the homeless? Thankfully, concerned citizens groups are marshalling support for these urban wayfarers, as the following headlines show...

The Salvation Army is encouraging home-less people to call home for Mother's Day.

Telephones will be available to make the free calls May 14 between 4-5 p.m. at 423 W. Third South, in the northeast section of the building.

Nudist Group Donates Clothing for Victims

Humph...easy for them.

No Need to Kill Poor; They're Killing Themselves

Why not kill the rich instead? There's fewer of them and it won't take as long.

Everyone knows that the entrepreneurial spirit is what has made America great. And nowhere is this spirit more in evidence than in the wide range of products being offered today's consumers. You may not *think* you want that macramé life preserver or those neon dentures, but think again— there's a great big world out there waiting to be bought!

HAVE I GOT A DEAL FOR YOU

mothers and dads everywhere will love it…

Copy-Tot

The Copy-Tot™ process was **developed for babies by a doctor,** for your use at home. Through extensive research and testing, this process was proven simple enough for anyone to do. The basic molding ingredients are clinically pure and have been in use for more than 50 years.

Capture sweet moments for grandparents

A Copy-Tot™ gift is a precious and unique reminder of their grandchild…a gift they'll treasure forever!

Copy-Tots™ are adorable with the Bronzit™ finish or a natural satin finish. Makes a tabletop keepsake, paperweight or even a penholder. Each kit includes enough Bronzit™ to put a beautiful, lasting bronze finish on your baby's casting…**plus** a Bronzit™ finish for your baby's first shoe …a delightful matched set!

♥**American Baby Products**
LINCOLN, NEBRASKA

Babies are tickled, too…they think it was invented just for their entertainment. In a minute, details are picked up, even from baby's wiggling hand or foot, in the rubbery casting mold.
It's so easy, it's on U.S. Patent Pending status.

(4 easy steps on the back)

…a one-of-a-kind casting kit…

…**FREE Bronzit™ finishing kit** with enough material to give a lasting bronze finish to your Copy-Tot™ and to baby's first shoe.

…**FREE Baby Fingerprint Protector™ kit** …the best way to keep a record of your baby's **only** permanent identifying characteristic…fingerprints!

…**Everything for do-it-at-home** cast copies that will look professional and last for generations.

TOTAL HAPPINESS GUARANTEE:
If, for any reason you're not entirely happy with Copy-Tot™, you may keep the double-use Bronzit™ finisher kit and the Baby Fingerprint Protector™ kit…and get your money back!

At $12.95 Copy-Tot™ is a never-before value…so little invested…such giant returns in sweet memories.
For immediate order or more information …*Call Toll Free.*

What greater gift than the gift of foot?

CUSTOM BUTCHERING
— Monday thru Friday By Appointment —

LOCKER BOX RENTAL

Home Killed Freezer Beef
Sold by hanging wt., Cutting, Wrapping & Freezing FREE

Front Qtrs. $1.29 - Hind Qtrs. $1.69 - Half $1.45

Don't let the grandparents in the last ad see this...

"Other 'stuff' "?
Hey, that wouldn't be a
manure cone, would it?

New In Your Area 475-POOP
P.O. Box 23164

CANINE CLEANERS

" Let Us Do Your Dirty Work"

FOR ONLY $5.00 PER WEEK, WE'LL CLEAN UP AFTER YOUR FAVORITE FRIEND.*

Plenty of room for advancement. Become the #2 man!

$5.00 VCR TUNE-UP

(Reg. $45.00 In Shop)

WITH PURCHASE OF ANY 2 LARGE SANDWICHES

We will clean: Video Head, Audio Head, Control Head, Erase Head, Tape Guide and Adjust Tracking and Tape Pad If Needed.

Big John's Sandwich & VCR Repair

AB138/FMA

Expires 5-30-89.

Here's your problem, sir. Your tape spool is clogged with mayonnaise.

TRULY AFFORDABLE EUROPEAN STYLING

POWER WINDOWS OPTIONAL!!

PEUGEOT

Yeah, but what about the disk player and leather interior?

All right,
here's my copy of the ad.
Give me one million gyros
and two with no sauce.

173

Free personalized checks.
Free travelers' checks.
Free money orders.
Free cashier's checks.
Free notary services.
Free safe deposit boxes:
Free registered keychain.
$15,000 insurance policy:
Itemized monthly statements.
No minimum balance.
No catch.

All for $3 a month.

No bank gives you so much more for so much less, than Southern Federal. People on the go want more, need more, expect more. So we make it easy, with Bonus Plus Checking.

The Plus? How about a ½-point discount on consumer loan interest? (Our holiday gift idea—spend less by taking out a loan with rates lower than most stores and credit cards. With the Bonus Plus discount, this could be your least expensive holiday season ever!)

Bonus Plus Checking, just $3 at Southern Federal. Shop around and you'll see the dollars and sense that banking with us can make.

can do!

SOUTHERN FEDERAL BANK FOR SAVINGS

Gee, look at all the free stuff
you get for only $3 a month.
Imagine if you had to pay money?

Yeah, they've got great buys.
I went last year and
the year before.

I know rust is
a big problem
in *our* family.

No comment.

First drinking . . .
now nude women.
What are these kids
going to do when
school is *out*?

COMPLETE FUNERAL

- FREE PICK-UP
- FREE EMBALMING
- FREE METAL CASKET
- FREE VIEWING
- ONE LIMOUSINE FREE

$999⁰⁰

DUVAL COUNTY ONLY
GOOD THRU JUNE 30

"PLEASE BRING
NEWSPAPER AD
WITH YOU."

TOSTON-LA FRANS FUNERAL HOME
BEAVER ST.   PH.

Remember, nobody buried without ad...

MONUMENTS

$328

Complete, including
inscription, delivery
and installation
at local cemetery.

ANDERSEN
JOSEPH

Choice of 16 designs.
Full size 400 lb., Grade
A Vermont Granite. Lifetime replacement guarantee.

Granite bases extra. as
regulated by cemetery

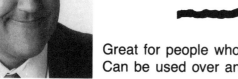

Great for people who believe in reincarnation
Can be used over and over again.

Now which one of these people is trying to make it a pleasant experience for the other?

Oh, go ahead. Treat yourself. You only live once.

Mother's Day SALE

Prices Good Through Saturday, May 27

S4S Radial
Goodyear Quality At Budget Prices

$29.95
P155/80R13 Whitewall
With Old Tire

WHITEWALL SIZE	EVERYDAY LOW PRICE With Old Tire	WHITEWALL SIZE	EVERYDAY LOW PRICE With Old Tire
P185/75R14		P205/75R15	$45.95
P195/75R14		P215/75R15	
P205/75R14		P225/75R15	

Tiempo Radial
Steel Belted Strength...
Smooth, Comfortable Ride

$36.95
P155/80R13 Whitewall
With Old Tire

WHITEWALL SIZE	EVERYDAY LOW PRICE With Old Tire	WHITEWALL SIZE	EVERYDAY LOW PRICE With Old Tire
P165/80R13	$41.95	P205/75R15	
P185/80R13	$45.95	P215/75R15	$40.95
P185/75R14	$49.95	P225/75R15	$43.95
P195/75R14	$43.95	P235/75R15	$44.95
P205/75R14			

Save on G–Metric Radial
For Small Cars & Imports

$29.95

Maybe Mom will like this better than those power tools I got her last year.

HAPPY HOLIDAYS!

*FREE HOUR OF SHOOTING
*FREE GUN RENTALS
WITH THIS AD & PURCHASE OF 100 RNDS RELOADS

LOW HOURLY RATES...PLUS MEMBERSHIPS AVAIL!
OPEN TO THE PUBLIC 7 DAYS TIL 11 PM!
TUESDAY IS LADIES DAY... FREE RANGE TIME!

FIRING-LINE
INDOOR	SHOOTING	RANGES
NORTHRIDGE	HUNTINGTON BEACH	BREA

LOW HOURLY RATES...OPEN TO THE PUBLIC 7 DAYS TIL 11 PM

What better gift this holiday season: the gift of lead.

FATHER'S DAY

at the

Oyster Reef

Our Regular Menu • 11:30 AM To 10 PM
Casual Dining Over The Water
By The Boats

Complimentary Glass Of Champagne
And A <u>Hooker</u> For Dad

FOR RESERVATIONS, ████████

████████ **EMBARCADERO   OAKLAND**

Why do I think this place is booked up already?

BON APPÉTIT!

Tired of that same old diet of tofu and oat bran? Well, here's some good eatin' that's sure to please the palate (and, we hear, low in cholesterol, too)...

Ants take a long time to cook in microwave

But well worth the wait.

ISU makes cow chips latest snack

ISU adds beef to corn chips to make a light, crunchy snack

The market for beefed up corn chips has a very bullish outlook, according to one Iowa State researcher.

~~Ricardo Mattos~~, professor of animal science, said the U.S. snack food market is ready for ISU's latest culinary development — the beef-corn snack chip.

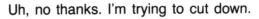

Uh, no thanks. I'm trying to cut down.

Do neat stuff like drinking sewer lice, teachers urged

Make a worm farm. Implode an aluminum can. Drink sewer lice. Carve rubber stamps out of erasers. Let pill bugs race. Launch a rocket.

Those stunts may read like a list penned by a vengeful delinquent, but they're actually a few teaching tools about 30 science teachers from around the state will explain during "Science on Saturday" from 8 a.m. to 3:30 p.m. Saturday at Memorial High

Here's an argument against tenure.

US says insect parts, rat hair are OK in food

Washington, D.C. —AP— Insect parts, rodent hairs and maggots don't sound appetizing, but when tossed with a salad, churned up in tomato sauce or baked in bread they're not bad at all, the government says.

But how do they taste with cow chips?

Nothing fishy about this

Spam sushi's a hit at S.J. restaurant

You wonder why more and more people are eating at home?

2 KIDS
2 HAMBURGERS
2 FRIES

$2⁰⁰

NO LIMIT

Please Present
Coupon When Ordering.
One Coupon Per Customer
No Other Discounts Apply.
Good At All Participating
Burger King Locations

EXPIRES APRIL 14th, 1989

BURGER KING®

Located across the street from
the United Methodist Church.

Pet cooking contest
coming to Highland

More than $1,000 in prizes will be at stake
when Pet Inc. and the City of Highland sponsor
the Pet Palate Pleasers 2nd Annual Cooking
Contest.

Uh, excuse me, can I use your dog basting brush?

HAMPTON - <u>The Hampton United Methodist Church</u> will sponsor a Harvest Supper on Saturday, October 1. The dinner will be served in two seatings: one at 5 p.m. and one at 6:30 p.m. Reservations are required and may be made by contacting the church office at 926-2702.

<u>The menu for the evening will be a traditional New England boiled sinner,</u> rolls, homemade apple pie, coffee, tea and cider. Admission is - Adults $6.75, children age 6 to 11 - $3.75, children under the age of 6 are admitted free.

Boy, and you thought Southern Baptists were strict.

Preview
of
Events

Chicken Dinner

Hibben United Methodist Church will sponsor a barbecue chicken dinner on Saturday, March 2, from 4 to 7 p.m. at the church on Coleman Boulevard. Take-outs will be available. Adults, $4.50, children 12 and under, $2.50, children under five free if eaten in dining room.

Gosh, I'm hungry.
Hand me that plate
of preschoolers, will you?

187

$9.95?! I can eat kids
for free at the
United Methodist Church.

Holiday Inn
Thanksgiving Day Menu
Buffet

ROAST TURKEY   CORN
PORK LOIN   GREEN BEANS
BAKED CHILDREN   GIBLET GRAVY
DRESSING   CRANBERRY
BAKED SWEET   SAUCE
    POTATOES   PUMPKIN PIE
MASHED POTATOES   ASSORTED CAKES

Private & Semi-private Dining

(RESERVATIONS NECESSARY)
FOR GROUPS OF 8 OR MORE!

* WHOLE TURKEY   DRESSING
MASHED POTATOES   CANDIED YAMS
GREEN BEANS   CORN
GIBLET GRAVY   CRANBERRY SAUCE
PUMPKIN PIES   CHERRY PIES

All Served Family Style

* One turkey will feed
approx. 10 people

$9.95 Per Person

HOLIDOME INDOOR RECREATION CENTER

Holiday Inn

MARION CONVENTION CENTER

School lunch menu . . .

Monday, Dec. 5
Baked chicken nuggets w. sweet & sour sauce, oven fried potatoes, carrots & celery stix, chilled pineapple tid-bits, milk

Tuesday, Dec. 6
Chilled fruit juice, grilled cheeseburger on a roll w. ketchup, pickles & chips, chilled pears, milk

Wednesday, Dec. 7
Submarine sandwich on French Bread w. sliced meats, cheese, lettuce, tomatoes & pickles, oven fried potatoes, strawberry jello w. topping, milk

Thursday, Dec. 8
Cup of children w. rice soup, cheese/tomato pizza, vegetable salad w. dressing, chilled peaches, milk

Friday, Dec. 9
Roast turkey w. gravy, whipped potatoes, sliced carrots & peas, cranberry sauce, bread & butter, chilled fruit cocktail, milk

---

The United Methodist Church is still the best deal in town.

7

If you thought death was the end of your fiduciary responsibilities, that you could rest in peace and not have to worry about keeping up appearances, think again...

THE TROUBLE WITH BEING DEAD

City wants Dead
to pay for cleanup

It's about time. They've been lying around long enough.

Teacher Dies;
Board Accepts
His Resignation

Normally we wouldn't, but I guess this time it's okay.

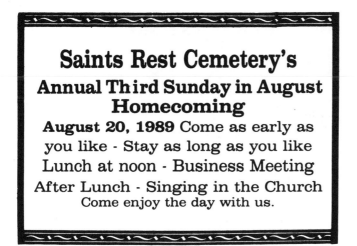

Saints Rest Cemetery's

Annual Third Sunday in August Homecoming

August 20, 1989 Come as early as you like - Stay as long as you like

Lunch at noon - Business Meeting

After Lunch - Singing in the Church
Come enjoy the day with us.

Wouldn't Halloween be a more appropriate time for this event?

You can still bury grandpa out back

You mean, we don't have to wait till he's dead?

Man reports wife's death —after game

Police questioning delay following fatal shooting

A Clayton County man told police his wife shot herself in the head after an argument Sunday, but he decided to go to his mother-in-law's house to watch the Super Bowl instead of reporting her death, officers said.

Yeah . . . so?

'Dead' woman doesn't recall what happened

All right, we're going to go over it one more time, and I'll sit here all night if I have to...

Mortuary adds drive-through
Mourners pay their final respects without having to leave their cars

Gee, I wonder if this is in L.A.?

New Stupid Way to Die Discovered

DANBURY, N.H. — An empty beer keg thrown onto a campfire exploded yesterday, killing a man at his birthday party in the second such death reported this month.

It's amazing how many new discoveries are made every day.

Woman Leaps To Death at Shea Stadium

New York

A woman climbed to the top of the right-field foul pole at empty Shea Stadium yesterday and jumped 120 feet to her death on the playing field, police said.

The woman, estimated to be between 30 and 40 years old, landed in what would be foul territory during a game. She was pronounced dead at the scene.

A foul? So she may have to jump again.

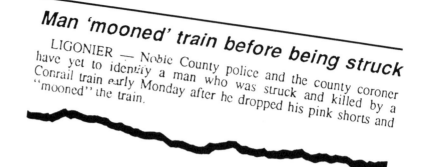

Man 'mooned' train before being struck

LIGONIER — Noble County police and the county coroner have yet to identify a man who was struck and killed by a Conrail train early Monday after he dropped his pink shorts and "mooned" the train.

Attention: hemorrhoid sufferers.

2 Rich Tennesseans' Deaths Pump $9 Into State Coffers

Oh, sure, the $9 looks good now, but once you deduct inheritance taxes and lawyers' fees...

8

For many, it's the favorite part of the evening newspaper—the section where you can get a line on that '65 Buick you've been wanting, check if they're any new listings for unskilled laborers, or look for a buyer for those 30 metric tons of solid toxic waste sitting behind your asbestos factory. What are we talking about? Well, the classifieds, of course...

CLASSIFY THIS, WILL YOU?

WANT ADS

Must sell volume 1 of headline book to buy Volume 2. No reasonable offer refused. DESPERATE.

**Thinking about
Selling Those No Longer
Needed Items?**

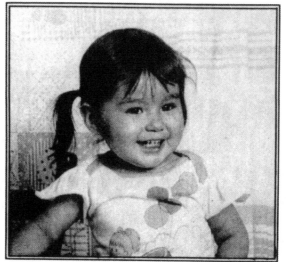

**Give The A-J Classifieds
A Try At A Price
You Can Afford.**

**DIVORCE SALE 1444 LOVERS LANE, April 29
8 AM to 5 PM - Furniture & Misc.**

Some people just can't
handle the pressure, I guess.

USED REAR ENDS
For most cars and light trucks,
$65 or $149.95 Installed.

And I'm sure it was owned by a little old lady
who only sat on it in church on Sunday...

**TRADE dental work for car or anything
of value. 284-0272**

How about a used rear end?

GRANDMOTHER WILL babysit 205 year old in her Stuart home.

205 year olds? Don't these kids have older brothers and sisters to take care of them?

PERSON to help wash windows. Send resume to P.O. Box ████, Williamsport, PA ████

After I graduated from Harvard, I went to the Wharton School of Business—plus I own my own rag.

RECEPTIONIST/LAW FIRM
$189,000 YR + BONUS

Greet important visitors, schedule appointments & answer phones on beautiful executive floor of top Chicago client law firm. 9 to 5; 5 days. Must have excellent personality, nice appearance & work well in a fast paced atmosphere. 100% public contact.

$189,000 a year...hmmm, but what about the bonus?

CHICKEN SEXER. To separate chicks by sex using the vent method to examine for presence or absence of male eminence. Require 1 year experience.

Do you think this is how the Colonel got started?

201

Alaska Airlines . . . swimming . . . .
It's not the swimming that bothers me,
it's breaking through that ice.

F96. Love dogs? Write to this lonely widow. She is 49, 150lbs, changeable eyes, financially secure, high morals, non-drinker, non-drugs. MAF40603B

Is this the *best* way to phrase your ad?

Courts

COUNTY COURT-AT-LAW NO. 1
Judge Weldon Copeland, presiding
Criminal Docket
Dispositions
1/11/89

Roger Dale ▓▓▓▓, guilty of overweight. Fined $113.50.

Guilty of being overweight?! Good thing he wasn't wearing plaid pants and white shoes— he could've gotten jail time.

203

Say this one three times, real fast...

You get
what you pay for.

9

Occasionally, we see headlines so thoroughly tasteless,
so inappropriate, that we just have to say:

NO COMMENT

Man stuck on toilet; stool suspected

Once-sagging cloth diaper industry saved by full dumps

Environmental concerns and other factors are creating a "substantial shift back to cloth diapers," the president of a diaper service which serves Terre Haute said Friday.

Moorpark residents enjoy a communal dump

All good couches must be laid to rest — in a place other than the backyard or the garage — sooner or later.

So must busted chairs and broken washing machines.

And several items such as these were finally thrown away Saturday during Moorpark's Neighborhood Cleanup Program.

Oshkosh sued for injury over runaway outhouse

An Oshkosh man is suing the city of Oshkosh for injuries sustained when he was hit by a runaway outhouse during last summer's Sawdust Daze celebration.

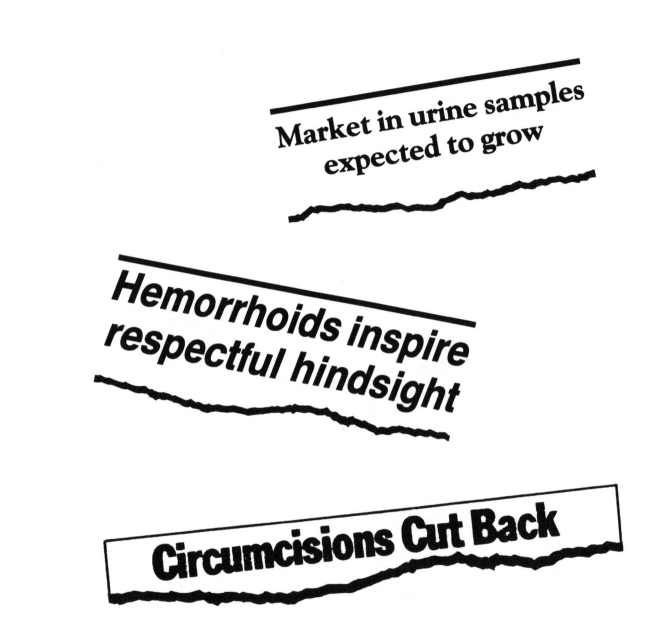

Market in urine samples
expected to grow

Hemorrhoids inspire
respectful hindsight

Circumcisions Cut Back

STOP THE PRESSES!

We live in an exciting era—one rife with discoveries, breakthroughs, and insights. Why, it seems hardly a day passes without some important finding being published. Take these headlines, for example...

Duh...

Blow to head is common cause of brain injury

Low pay reason for poverty, study says

Double duh...

July 4, 1776, Was 'A Turning Point In History,' President Says

Who says politicians are afraid to go out on a limb?

"You mean it won't drain out the top?" department:

Drain plug located at bottom

Don't leave kids alone with molester

Am I glad I read the paper today.

Radioactive Dump Could Be Hazard

Yeah, but only for the next three million years.

Health Tip

Studies indicate fat intake affects obesity

Thanks for the tip.

Storm delayed by bad weather

Another picnic ruined.

Married women can enter the Mrs. Arizona pageant

Then single women should be able to enter the Miss Arizona pageant.

Unfair. Men should be able to find out if they're pregnant, too.

Experts Are Sure the Dow Will Either Rise or Decline

Boy, business forecasting is an exact science, isn't it?

FORBIDDEN FRUIT

We've all seen it—that come-hither headline that taunts with its innuendo. The kind that has you craning your neck to read the paper of the person in front of you, sure that a certain naughty subject is about to be discussed. Somehow, though, like that officemate who gives you a suggestive wink at the coffee machine, it always seems to promise more than it delivers...

And you thought
Hef's was wild.

Vets called in to cool down duck sex orgy

HOBART, Australia (AFP) — Authorities had to drug 16 sex-crazed drakes who were drowning their lady-love ducks in aquatic orgies on Launceston City Park pond.

"Their heavy love-making in the pond was just too much for the little ducks and the weight of numbers drowned them," said a Launceston city council spokesman.

State to punish duck violators

You've got to be pretty sick to violate a duck.

Sex with weeds may be hurting plant genetics

I've heard of people talking to their plants, but this is ridiculous.

Sperm-donor project may boost chicken industry

What? No dinner and movie first?

Bush orders Army troops to U.S. Virgins

Gee, kinda makes you want to put on a uniform, doesn't it?

"Why Congress is fighting to keep our bases open" department:

If U.S. bases close, prostitutes would likely be out of work

Hooker Quits
Mason Position

I guess it can be really rough on the elbows.

Hooker leaves partners hanging

You think this has anything to do with the Mason position?

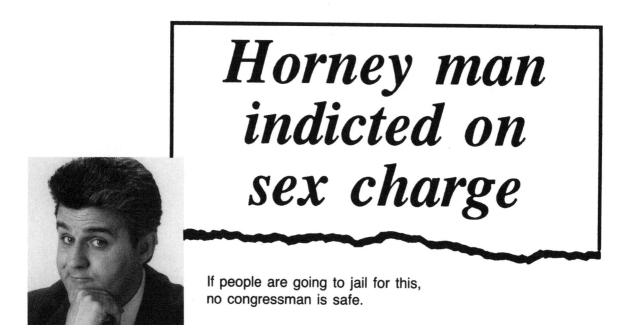

Horney man indicted on sex charge

If people are going to jail for this,
no congressman is safe.

If Voters Approve, Boys Town Will Buy Orphanage With Girls

Party... party... party...

And the thing I like about it, it's so subtle.

I've heard of phony ways to meet women but this one takes the cake.

Wanted: Women To Test New Condom

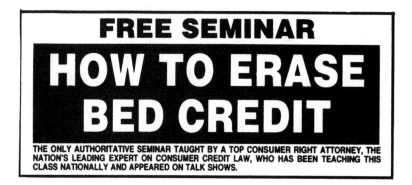

FREE SEMINAR

HOW TO ERASE BED CREDIT

THE ONLY AUTHORITATIVE SEMINAR TAUGHT BY A TOP CONSUMER RIGHT ATTORNEY, THE NATION'S LEADING EXPERT ON CONSUMER CREDIT LAW, WHO HAS BEEN TEACHING THIS CLASS NATIONALLY AND APPEARED ON TALK SHOWS.

Good idea, who hasn't had a few of those they wouldn't mind erasing?

San Luis Obispo

Police were called Sunday night to the Economy Motel by a man having trouble getting his wife out of a pair of handcuffs.

No other information was available.

★ ★ ★

No other information is needed.

Good Ol' Days

April 1, 1981

Amy Marie was born to Randy and Robin and Jessica Faulk on March 27.

Ah...life on the commune.

PHOTO FOUL-UPS

By far, my favorite journalistic gaffes are weird photo/headline juxtapositions that, though unintentional, conjure up frightening thoughts. See if these foul-ups don't give you a few shudders...

New drug brightens aging brain

WASHINGTON (AP) — Brains dulled by age may be restored to the quick brightness of youth by a new drug developed for treatment of stroke, Chicago researchers report in a study published today.

President George Bush

Hey, do you think the guy who positioned this photo is a Democrat?

Quayle dodges shots off trail

COFFEYVILLE JOURNAL

Sacramento's Newest Luxury Hotel

Riverboat Delta King

Hmmm, I wonder if rooms below the waterline are cheaper?

227

Firefighting tactics in fatal blaze will get close look

I hope so. The savings in gas and oil don't begin to make up for the peanut bills.

Rabbits Nibbling Away Big Chunks of Australia

CANBERRA, Australia—This country is at war with 200 million rabbits nibbling their way at great expense across vast tracts of land.

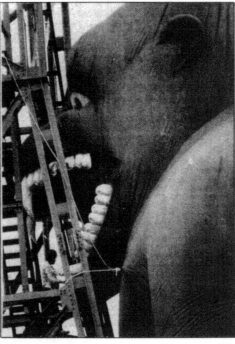

UPI

Inflated appearance—Worker inflates a 2,000-pound, 70-foot-tall replica of King Kong attached to 300-foot-high observation tower at Six Flags Over Texas amusement park near Dallas.

Where's Crocodile Dundee when you need him?

From the "Bill, we think you'll be better off behind the grill instead of working the customer window" department:

Handicapped find job help

Biology instructor David Sutton adjusted an octopus outfit worn by Tim Shipley, 17

Roaming Back Roads of Romania by Rental Car

BUCHAREST, Romania—When a friend and I booked our 10-day Romania self-drive package it seemed too good to be true: rental car with unlimited mileage, insurance, even coupons for 70 liters of gas, hotels, two meals a day, visa, transfers and assistance on arrival and departure. All for just over $600 each.

JOYCE M. DALTON

But do you get unlimited mileage?

Secret shuttle flight has been flawless

These are the possible landing sites for the shuttle.

ASSOCIATED PRESS

Are these *really* the possible landing sites for the shuttle?
It looks like the parking lot is full.

Iran hangs 70 in drug crackdown

I don't think most of these guys mind being hung.
It's having their faces stuck through that board that bothers them.

"Funny, there was water here yesterday" department:

THE ARIZONA DAILY STAR

Travel plans changed

Although Hurricane Gilbert is expected to smash into the Gulf Coast about 1,000 miles southeast of Tucson, it is affecting some traveling Tucsonans.

PROPANE BLAST – This is one of two homes destroyed in a Tuesday afternoon blast in Fordyce. A local business also was damaged. Propane was accidentally fed into the city water system.

Exploding toilets no joke in Fordyce

So kids, remember that the next time you try to fool Dad with that exploding toilet gag.

From the "It's all relative" department:

Firefighters Larry Patterson and Jenny Lindgren look over the wreckage of a house under construction that was blown down by gusts Wednesday that reached 60 mph. No one was injured. The house is at 14656 Pratt St. in Woodbridge.

High winds cause minor damage

235

Kenneth P. Lambert/Journal

Moth control plans detailed

Wouldn't it be safer to just buy screens?

World leaders remember Hirohito

UPI

Copyright Houston Chronicle. Reprinted with permission.

Gee, do you think
Mickey stayed here
when he visited Hirohito?

From the "I think it's just mist" department:

Officials Deny Presence of Toxic Flames

SALT LAKE TRIBUNE

From the "How long have you lived at the North Pole?" department:

UPI

Illegal Farm Workers Rush to Beat Residency Deadline

From the "Exactly how hazy was it?" department:

Thunderbirds Stage Show At Norton A.F.B.

The U.S. Air Force Thunderbirds perform with hazy skies during yesterday's air show at Norton Air Force Base in San Bernardino.

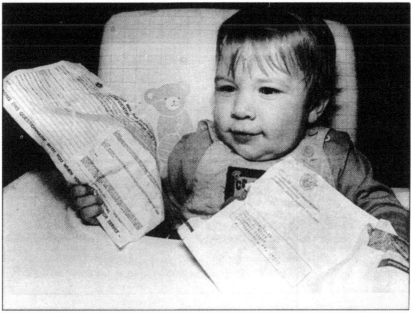

ASSOCIATED PRESS

Jury duty

Tyler Morey, 11 months old, holds a notice to report for jury
duty in Berkshire County, Mass.

Hey, it's cheaper
than day care.

241

KCC cracks down on gas leaks

From staff and wire reports
TOPEKA — On the heels of natural gas explosions in Kansas and Missouri, the Kansas Corporation Commission on Wednesday ordered utilities to beef up testing for natural gas leaks and replace service lines when leaks were detected.

You can start by closing that door.

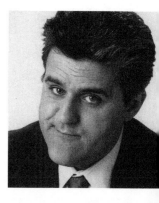

Coalition forms task force to combat crime at ATMs

Responding to increased consumer concern about the safety of automated teller machines, a coalition of bankers, manufacturers and trade groups has formed a task force on how to avoid ATM crime.

I'm sure you're *very* trustworthy, sir, but if you want to make a withdrawal, you'll have to bring Mr. Bruce Wayne down here himself.

Death I can handle.
It's losing those ski privileges
I'm worried about.

© DAVID H. FAUSS, Atlanta, GA

BRIAN MASCK/THE MUSKEGON CHRONICLE

HEADLINES III:
NOT THE MOVIE, STILL THE BOOK

COMPILED BY JAY LENO

WITH PHOTOGRAPHS BY JOSEPH DEL VALLE
AND CARTOONS BY JACK DAVIS

With the publication of the third book of HEADLINES, we would like to take this opportunity to thank you for your support of pediatric A.I.D.S. programs not only through your purchase of these books but by taking the time to send these headlines to Jay.

Please know that over the past three years, 100 percent of all the author's royalties from these books have gone directly to many organizations. Childrens' hospitals and related support programs throughout the country have been the beneficiary of your generosity.

You have made a difference.

Sincerely,

SAMUEL JARED KUSHNICK FOUNDATION

BRILLIANT DEDUCTIONS

With investigative techniques that rival Sherlock Holmes's, today's scientists are peeling back the layers of knowledge—arriving at undreamed-of discoveries. Take the following headlines, for example...

Smaller families require less food

So that would mean bigger families require more food? I'm confused.

Farmers buy most farmland

WASHINGTON — Through thick and thin, the biggest buyers of farmland are other farmers, says an Agriculture Department report.

Gee, I wonder what they do with it?

Ability to swim may save children from drowning

I guess we'll just have to use bigger weights.

Sewers are not good playgrounds

Sounds like just another overprotective mom.

Americans are unlikely to give up eating during recession

Jail crowding caused by increase in criminals, new study concludes

Let's not jump to any conclusions.

Panel hears specialist testify — women's breasts not like men's

I'd like more time to study this case.

DID I READ THAT RIGHT?

The job of the family newspaper is not to misdirect readers—as supermarket tabloids sometimes do—but inform. Occasionally, though, they just can't help it...

Attorneys don't want ban on lawyer-client sex

SACRAMENTO (AP) — California attorneys were ordered to draft rules limiting their sexual behavior after claims that a famed divorce attorney raped two clients, but critics say the proposed regulations are too liberal.

Now there's a shock.

Nuclear winter may not be so bad

Yeah, and playing in the sewer is a lot of fun, too.

Blind Cabbie Forced To Abandon Driving

Now he can go back to his day job as an umpire.

Bomb hit by library

Mimes banned for abusive language

CLEVELAND HEIGHTS—
The San Francisco Mime troupe was banned from performing at Heights High School after school officials said they didn't like the language used in the production.

It's not *what* they said, it's *how* they said it.

Ten Commandments declared obsolete by 'news king' Turner

TV mogul issues his own 10 rules

I guess if you've broken them all, they *are* obsolete.

State will poison rivers so it can count dead fish

Hey, this doesn't have anything to do with that "all-you-can-eat" fish fry, does it?

Train towed after collision with '83 Buick

PEEKSKILL — When a turbo-charged Amtrak engine slammed into ~~Clifford Austin~~ in his '83 Buick on Tuesday morning, ~~Clifford~~ was able to walk away.

The Buick suffered some damage to a front fender, but the locomotive was dead in its tracks.

It's a good thing it wasn't a '59 Cadillac.
Everybody on that train would have been killed!

"Girls will be girls" department: **Woman is pregnant, thanks to her sister**

Some men retain mental ability

Here's one feminists may dispute.

"Hey, wait a minute. I don't remember reading that in the catalogue" department:

Univ. Of Michigan Mulls Neutering Its Freshmen

Good luck trying to collect.

Post office paychecks get lost in mail

What goes around comes around.

Man pleads innocent to charges of sexual assault on horse

An Itawamba County man accused in a string of sexual assaults on Lee County horses pleaded innocent to four related charges at his arraignment Monday in Lee County Circuit Court.

▬▬▬▬▬▬▬▬▬▬▬▬▬▬▬▬, pleaded innocent to having intercourse with an animal, killing a quarter horse, grand larceny in connection with the abduction of a Shetland pony and destruction of private property in connection with another assault.

Animal-rights group to hold meeting at steakhouse

GREAT FALLS, Mont. (AP) — An animal-rights group that hopes to change Americans' meat-eating ways scheduled a meeting here today at the Black Angus steakhouse.

Before I begin the meeting, let me have two lamb chops, one New York sirloin, and a pork loin.

"Maybe you should grow a beard" department:

'Hole in face' sends man to hospital

████████, 21, of College Station was shot in the left side of his face while walking in the Highland Courts housing project about 10:30 p.m. Wednesday, but didn't realize he had "a hole in his face" until the following day, he told Little Rock police.

Solid Waste, Recycling to be Dinner Topic

Hey, why don't we meet at that steakhouse?

Woman unsure how she sat on pork chop bone

NASHVILLE — Julia ~~Schindarsky~~ is more careful about where she sits after doctors looking for cancer found a pork chop bone in her derriere.

Doctors removed the 4-'inch bone last October from the left cheek on her buttocks and estimate the bone had been there between five and 10 years.

"They thought it was a tumor, and instead of finding a tumor they found a pork chop bone," Mrs. ~~Schindarsky, 64, of Nashville~~ said recently.

The *good* news, ma'am, is that you don't have hemorrhoids...

Angry, jobless Santas picket mall after elf accused of lechery

West Seneca, N.Y.
Santa Claus walked a picket line Friday after a company that provides Santas was fired by mall managers because an elf allegedly made a suggestive comment to a store employee.

♪♪   ♪♪

Jingle bells, jingle bells, jingle all...

Customers didn't notice dead clerk

Excuse me, can you help me?...
Uh, excuse me...excuse me...

Teen births in Brevard up 17 percent, study says

Birth rate dropping among Brevard teens

This is what happens when you send two reporters to cover the same story.

Passenger trains hurt by lack of track

WASHINGTON — Passenger rail service across much of the country is being threatened by a lack of suitable track.

Uh-oh, what's that com—
Hey! Look out for that '83 Buick!!!

Gas chamber executions may be health hazard

You know, I think it's true.
Everyone who's used it is dead now.

Lead-Lined Coffins
Called Health Risk

Sydney

Australian funeral workers in New South Wales say they are prone to strain injuries because the state insists lead-lined coffins be used for above-ground interments.

"We've had back and shoulder injuries as well as hernias," said Lyle Pepper, head of the New South Wales Funeral and Allied Industries Union.

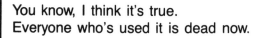

Gas chambers?
Lead-lined coffins?
Isn't there any safe place?

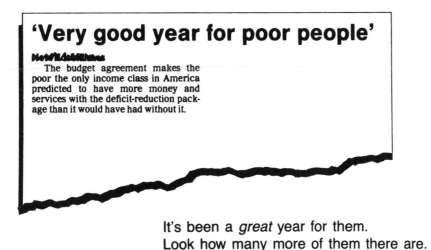

'Very good year for poor people'

The budget agreement makes the poor the only income class in America predicted to have more money and services with the deficit-reduction package than it would have had without it.

It's been a *great* year for them.
Look how many more of them there are.

Nude scene done tastefully in radio play

Turn up the volume, Martha, I think they're naked.

Thirteen years?
Who did the looking—
another turtle?

Missing turtle turns up after 13 years

LONDON (AP) — An Oriental soft shell turtle, presumed dead for 13 years, has been found alive and well in her compartment at a zoo in Devon, the curator says.

~~XXXXXXXX~~ said the turtle, who disappeared in 1976 from Paignton Zoo, 130 miles southwest of London, was found hiding in a silted pond after a gardener spotted her stealing meat. The turtle is now full size with a large, bobbing neck and a 12-inch grey, soft, pliant shell.

Zookeepers were amazed at its excellent condition especially since the turtle's primary diet is meat and there was no meat in the Tropical House until last week, when meat-eating birds arrived.

Iowa cemeteries are death traps

How many people have to die before we correct this problem?

Military Sealift Command Probes Munitions Mix-Up

WASHINGTON — The Military Sealift Command Monday was still investigating an incident in which 84 tons of munitions bound for the Middle East ended up at a **Port of New Orleans** shopping mall. ←

Hey, Bob, these cruise missiles—
do they go to Wicks & Things or Toys R Us?

MGM bounces checks, but says finances OK

Yeah, right, tell it to my landlord.

271

SMILES to Russell Bellamy and Brent Hertenlehner, both of Port Charlotte, who left their lunch to jump into a canal and save George Bauman, who was floating face-down. Hertenlehner pulled Bauman from the water and Bellamy administered CPR. Such unselfishness on the part of private citizens is commendable.

Imagine—leaving your lunch to save another human being.

72 jump into bed for world record

Has Madonna heard about this?

Dog was my co-pilot, driver says

SANTA CLARA, Calif. — This is a true story about bad eyes, a barking dog and life in the fast lane.

A visually impaired San Francisco man on Friday tried to convince a judge he wasn't driving solo in the commuter lane, arguing that his dog, Queenie, should count as a second person because she was helping him navigate.

Hey, didn't this guy used to be an umpire and a cabdriver?

Nothing destroyed in fire, but damage near $100,000

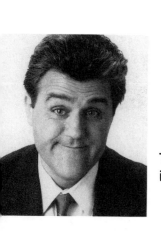

They were lucky. Imagine what it would have cost if something *had* been destroyed?

Squashed squirrels annoy drivers

ANNAPOLIS (AP) — Squirrels are being squashed in increasing numbers in Maryland and Virginia, annoying and frustrating motorists who try to avoid turning them into road pizza.

Get out of my way. I'm trying to get to the animal rights meeting at the steakhouse.

A MIND IS A TERRIBLE THING TO WASTE—OR IS IT?

Education, it's often said, is the foundation of a great society. Thus, the importance of school—you know, that place where young people go when things get dull at the mall? To all those dedicated cafeteria workers, crossing guards, and hygiene instructors—these headlines are for you...

"My school's gooder than yours" department:

WHERE

EXCELLANCE

IS

TRADITION

GLENBARD SOUTH HIGH SCHOOL
PARK BOULEVARD & BUTTERFIELD ROAD
GLEN ELLYN, ILLINOIS 60137
PHONE:

Peter J. Abruzzo, Principal

Reeding tutors needed

The Tooele Adult Education instructors need trained tutors to help adults learn to read.

Please apply at Glenbard South High School.

USPS Program Helps to "Stamp Out Literacy"

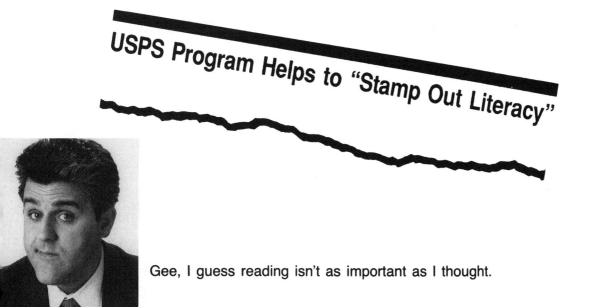

Gee, I guess reading isn't as important as I thought.

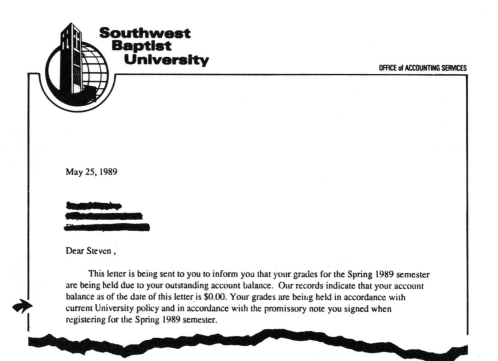

Southwest Baptist University

May 25, 1989

Dear Steven ,

    This letter is being sent to you to inform you that your grades for the Spring 1989 semester are being held due to your outstanding account balance. Our records indicate that your account balance as of the date of this letter is $0.00. Your grades are being held in accordance with current University policy and in accordance with the promissory note you signed when registering for the Spring 1989 semester.

It's not the amount of money. It's the principle involved.

East Principal Bans Student Mural About Censorship

Wait till he sees the sex ed mural.

Study finds that pupils who attend their classes score markedly better

Hey, you don't think this education thing is working, do you?

Iraq Invades Kuwait; Students May Lose Parking

The ravages of war can affect everyone.

THE CRIMINAL ELEMENT

Criminal vs. cop. It's a confrontation that occurs every day on our city streets: the diabolical criminal, willing to stop at nothing, pitted against our men in blue, schooled in the latest crime-fighting techniques. The following headlines tell the dramatic story...

Cops halt doughnut shop robbery

Hey, why not? They were there anyway.

Deputy implicated in doughnut theft

Well, Your Honor,
he did have a *glazed* look in his eye.

Hostage-taker kills self; police shoot each other

The first rule of police work:
never get emotionally involved with a criminal.

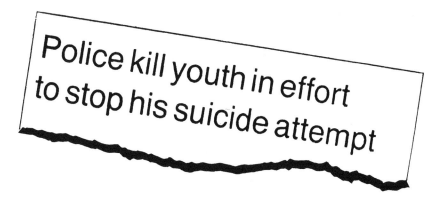

Police kill youth in effort to stop his suicide attempt

They had no choice.
Suicide is against the law.

(283)

Fingerprints help cops crack case of the busted piggy bank

David ███████ didn't exactly get caught with his hand in the cookie jar, police say, just with his fingers on the piggy bank.

The Passaic roofer was accused recently of breaking into a Garfield home, ransacking the owner's bedroom, and breaking a porcelain piggy bank cherished by a 3-year-old girl, police say.

He then took the girl's savings, about $5 in pennies, nickels, dimes, and quarters, police say.

"It was a difficult situation; you feel bad for the kid," said Capt. Al

Now, listen to me, Johnson. The mayor's on my back, the newspapers are hounding me. I want answers on this case, and I want them *now*.

"Is that a gun or are you happy to see me?" department:

Pants Bulge Provides No Basis for Search

A DIVIDED appellate court has overturned a Manhattan man's drug possession conviction, ruling that an undefined bulge in the man's pants was not suspicious enough to justify a police officer's search and discovery of a bag of cocaine.

"I won't say anything if you don't" department:

Deputy shoots self in butt

URBANA — A Clark County Sheriff's deputy accidently shot himself in his right buttock while attempting to conceal his gun behind his back before searching a Champaign County residence Thursday night.

Testicle cargo seized

Ow... I'll talk! I'll talk!

Naked man trying to buy soda arrested for stealing car

MIDDLESEX—A naked Massachusetts man trying to buy soda at Rick's Sunoco Station was arrested after police discovered the car he was driving was stolen in Brooklyn.

Was it diet soda or regular?

Police kill 2 pit bulls trying to eat live cow

MANNINGTON, W.Va. — Two pit bulls trying to devour a 600-pound cow alive were downed by police bullets as they rushed to attack two officers, collapsing dead just short of their targets.

Basically, they're good little dogs.

Eatery worker arrested after allegedly blowing nose in officer's burger

A 20-year-old fast-food worker has been arrested after he allegedly blew his nose into a hamburger that he served to a Phoenix police officer and then laughed about it.

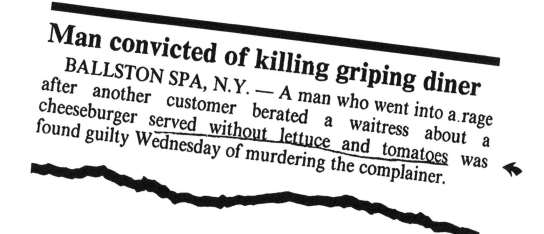

Man convicted of killing griping diner

BALLSTON SPA, N.Y. — A man who went into a rage after another customer berated a waitress about a cheeseburger served without lettuce and tomatoes was found guilty Wednesday of murdering the complainer.

I bet they won't forget the lettuce and tomato next time.

Theft suspect unable to take off with stolen pigeons in his pants

BALTIMORE — A police officer stopped a man who was walking oddly down the street with bulging pants and found that he had 21 live homing pigeons stuffed in his clothes.

Have the Wright brothers heard of this?

Toy gun scares robber using toy gun

Rochester police on Friday arrested a toy-gun-toting robber who was scared off by the toy gun of one of his victims and then hit on the head by a bat-wielding neighbor.

Good thing they didn't shoot each other. They both could have gotten soaking wet.

Suspect in bank holdups driven by cocaine habit

Police said  case is another sad story of crime driven by drug addiction. They described the Winslow Avenue man as a confused and nervous bandit who once left a bank empty-handed because a teller told him he needed to have an account at the branch in order to rob it.

I wonder if this is the same guy who got scared by that toy gun?

Young bunglers try to steal a van filled with policemen

LAKELAND, Fla. — Of all the cars and trucks in the mall's parking lot on one of the year's busiest shopping days, a quartet of would-be car thieves picked on a police surveillance van.

"It was hard to keep from laughing," said Mike Link, one of three officers hiding in the back of the van Saturday when one of the group climbed inside and turned the key.

Boy, and you thought the last guy was stupid.

IRS says it killed four men

You ever notice how these stories
always come out around tax time?

Several Items Reported
Stolen From Empty Store

Do you think this is what the typical police report
looks like in Moscow?

Man allegedly beaten by woman with a frozen fish

Con Sends Death Notes to Judges After Learning to Write in Prison

He's hooked on phonics, Your Honor.

Woman sits on gun that shoots her

An Issaquah-area woman sat on a gun that shot her on May 15, according to police and fire records.

The 25-year-old woman, who lives between Issaquah and Renton, returned home from a restaurant and was sitting on her bed when she heard a large noise and felt a sharp pain in her rear end, police report. Police discov-ered she had sat on a .22 caliber pistol that was on the bed.

Do you think she mistook it for a pork chop?
(See page 264.)

"A large, shaggy dog was seen lurking in the area" department:

Cat killed by pellet

A Bethlehem cat was killed with a high-powered pellet gun Thursday afternoon, police said.

➹ Bethlehem police investigators are considering the feline's death suspicious.

Police Beat

Monday morning, a Mt. Desert Street store reported that a white cat had entered the store on three occasions and taken a cat-nip mouse each time. The cat was described as white and wearing a flea color.

A large, shaggy dog was seen lurking in the area.

296

Bucks man admits attacking house, must go to Florida

Kevin ~~Michael Burge~~, who pleaded guilty yesterday to attacking his former neighbor's home with a chain saw, will be paroled from prison next week and required to live with his parents in Florida.

Attack a house, go to Florida. It's the law.

"Just keep digging" department:

PENN TOWNSHIP POLICE
FRIDAY

8:30 a.m. A tombstone bearing the name of Sarah J. Moul was found near Hanover Brands. Police are attempting to locate the owner.

PARENTAL GUIDANCE SUGGESTED

With television and radio broadcasting Madonna videos, 2 Live Crew songs, and Depends commercials, those in the newspaper biz can be forgiven if their headlines veer occasionally toward the risqué. But we should be no less vigilant in protecting our children from headlines like the following...

Sorority girls go up and down to benefit Heart Association

Tell me about it.

Penile implants raise hopes

Is this really the best way to phrase this sentence?

Experts test 16,000 condoms

I guess Warren Beatty and Ted Kennedy were busy.

Condom instructions require college-level reading ability

Where are the Cliff notes when you really need them?

Concord sued over cameras in the potty

SAN FRANCISCO (AP) — The City of Concord has been sued for $30 million because a video camera was placed in the police station men's room.

The suit was filed in U.S. District Court on Tuesday by 29 current and former Concord police officers and civilian employees.

The department installed a hidden video camera above a urinal in 1986, hoping to identify the person who clogged it several times with toilet paper.

Uh, I think we can skip looking at Exhibit A, Your Honor.

Man trapped in outhouse overnight 'in ugly mood'

LAWRENCE, Kan. (AP) — After spending a hot summer night at the bottom of an outhouse toilet, a man was pulled free Friday morning unhurt "but in a pretty ugly mood," authorities said.

If we'd had a camera in that potty, this never would have happened.

Investigators crack down on toilet paper offenders

ATLANTIC CITY — The toilet paper cops are making sure the streets of Atlantic City stay clean.

~~Joe Keyson~~ of City Bargains on Atlantic Avenue got more than he bargained for when he tried to sell unmarked rolls of toilet paper and paper towels.

"That's a violation for sure," said Nat Parker, assistant superintendent of the Atlantic City Division of Weights and Measures. "The consumer must know what he's getting."

It's about time they stopped harassing the drug dealers and murderers and went after the real criminals.

IF WE DON'T HAVE IT, WE'LL GET IT!

Recent visitors to the Soviet Union report shocking scarcities—shoe stores with no shoes, butcher shops with no meat. How fortunate that Americans can choose from the bountiful bargains offered here...

I don't even want to
know what this is.

If Timmy is going to school with anything less than an M-1 carbine, he could be unprepared. Don't let your child fall behind.

Do you pay extra
for the hot wax?

Gee, do you have one that responds to smoke?

Let me have two jars of strained carrots and a bottle of Jack Daniels. It's for our three-month-old.

"Revolutionary breakthrough—never needs ironing" department:

Great Buys For Christmas & New Years

New Poly Tuxedos
regularly $175 $129
New All Wood Tuxedos
Values from $250-$595 $199 to $299

For Location Nearest You

HiKEN

FORMAL RENTALS

Nero's GROCERY
COAL & WOOD
SANDWICHES

Here's one way to get more roughage.

Dietrich W. Oellerich Jr., PC
Attorney At Law

10% OFF Free Consultation

Hwy 88, Hephzibah, GA.

Nah, my guy gives 20% off free consultations.

HALLOWEEN *Sale!*

OVER 1,000,000 ITEMS IN STOCK
10-60% DISCOUNTS ON EVERYTHING

More Styles Than Ever!

Over **200** Accessories, Jewelry and Weapon Choices! • **150** Masks • **100's** of Hats, Wigs and Makeup Disguises • Body Parts and Vermon! • Now More Than **175** Costumes and Kits • Paper Goods • Toys & Give Aways • Lights • Decorations • More!

NINJA TURTLE • JASON • FREDDY • BATHMAN ←

I'll bet the Bathman stuff is *really* discounted.

Forget surprising him.
Ambush him.

315

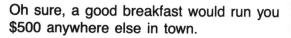

Why Would Anyone Eat Breakfast Any Place Else?

$299

No Coupon Necessary

...The Most Fantastic View in Town
...Absolutely Affordable
...All Breakfasts Cooked to Order
...Friendly & Fast Service

OUR DAILY BREAKFAST SPECIAL

2 Eggs, Bacon, Sausage, or Ham, Home Fries & Homemade Biscuits

Oh sure, a good breakfast would run you $500 anywhere else in town.

**"Don't go out of your way
on my account" department:**

"I can't wait to have the rabbi over for dinner" department:

Lose the whole summer?
Hey pal, if that's a
table saw they're using
you could lose
a lot more.

R.W. BY-PRODUCT CO.

Recyclers of Inedible
Restaurant Grease

Call for
Immediate Service

Boy, I'm getting hungry already.

WOMEN IN JAIL
Seek Boyfriends and Husbands

Introducing Aemrica's most exciting dateline—for women who will soon be released from jail ... and men who want to meet them!

Can you help them out? Do you want to meet a woman who will really appreciate being with you?

CALL NOW — WOMEN IN JAIL
1-███-███-███
THAT'S 1-900-███
THEY'RE GETTING OUT SOON
AND THEY NEED YOUR COMPANY.

$1 min., $2 the 1st. ADULTS ONLY

Hey, Mom, remember that Brinks job twenty years ago? Well, this is Susan and she...

THE COUPON TABLOID

DOUBLE DEAL *Pizza*

Laguna Lake Center

2 CALZONES
(Stuffed Italian Panties)
Ricotta & Mozzarella + 4 TOPPINGS

$10.39 Plus Tax

FREE DELIVERY!
ONE COUPON

with coupon
expires 1/16/91

Yum.

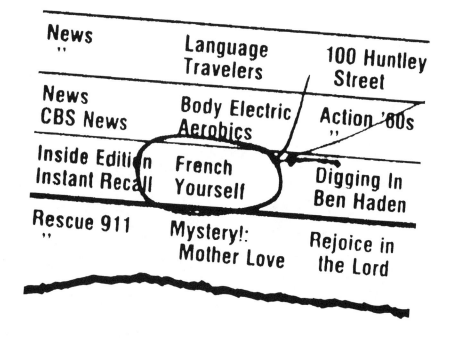

News	Language Travelers	100 Huntley Street
News CBS News	Body Electric Aerobics	Action '60s
Inside Edition Instant Recall	French Yourself	Digging In Ben Haden
Rescue 911	Mystery!: Mother Love	Rejoice in the Lord

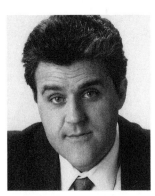

Sounds like the latest Madonna self-help video.

CEMETERY PLOTS
2 Butler County
Memorial Park, never
used, $2850. 8

How much for the used ones?

35, 40, Or 60 Watt

ORAL-B TOOTHBRUSH

Each

$1⁹⁹

I think I'll stick to my regular toothbrush, thanks.

"Hey, this sausage tastes funny" department:

Let Us Plan
Your Post Funeral
Luncheon
WINDSOR MILLS
RESTAURANT
(▬) ▬ ▬ ▬

What a great funeral. I'm stuffed.

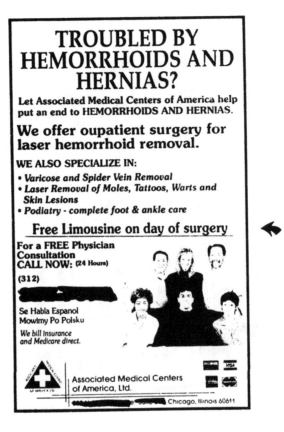

TROUBLED BY HEMORRHOIDS AND HERNIAS?

Let Associated Medical Centers of America help put an end to HEMORRHOIDS AND HERNIAS.

We offer oupatient surgery for laser hemorrhoid removal.

WE ALSO SPECIALIZE IN:
- *Varicose and Spider Vein Removal*
- *Laser Removal of Moles, Tattoos, Warts and Skin Lesions*
- *Podiatry - complete foot & ankle care*

Free Limousine on day of surgery

For a FREE Physician Consultation CALL NOW: (24 Hours)

(312) ███████

Se Habla Espanol
Mowimy Po Polsku

*We bill Insurance
and Medicare direct.*

Associated Medical Centers
of America, Ltd.

████████ Chicago, Illinois 60611

Hey, take it easy
over those speed
bumps, will you?

OUR GIFT TO YOU
and your family

Call our office within 20 days, and our gift to you will be a complete consultation, exam and x-rays (if needed) for $1.00 charge.

We welcome you and your family to join our practice of complete family dentistry and orthodontics. <u>We specialize in chickens,</u> financing available. Open 7 a.m. - 7 p.m. and Saturdays. Our staff will be complimented to have you choose our office for all your dental needs.

GUTHRIE DENTAL GROUP

Hello, Doctor.
My Rhode Island red has a serious overbite...

Of course it is. It's not about giving or helping someone less fortunate than you. It's about chewing.

CAST YOUR BALLOTS

Many of us envy the politician's life—traveling on junkets, squiring beautiful women around town, receiving kickbacks. But it has its downside, too, as the following headlines show...

White House takes shot at Democrats

A Kuwaiti guards a man identified as an Iraqi army major during questioning in Kuwait City Friday after the suspect was captured at a roadblock. Moments after this picture was taken, the photographer was asked to leave.

Looks like the campaign's starting to heat up.

Captors free Trinidad prime minister
40 still held as Robinson, shot in feet, agrees to step down

Now, be honest. Did you think he would have stepped down if he *hadn't* been shot in the foot?

Rockland incumbents lose; deceased candidate re-elected

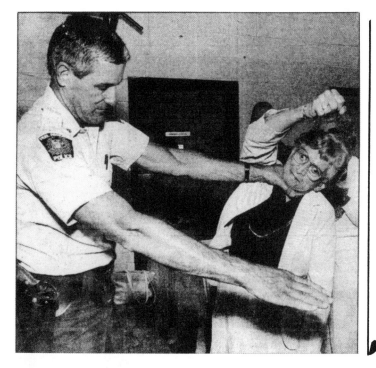

Alderman renews charge of harassment from colleague

Mom, I *told* you not to bother me at the office.

White supremacists stumping for top state offices in South

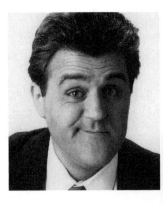

So I guess it's true, all white people do look alike.

A man holds back tears while another kneels on the ground outside the Imperial Palace in Tokyo early this morning.

Three state congressmen oppose 50% pay increase

You know, for a minute there I almost believed them.

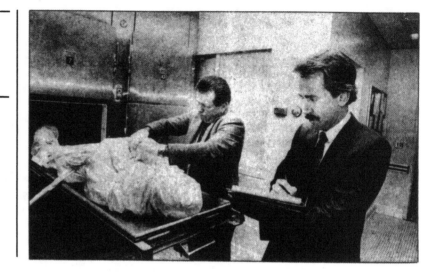

Hey, Doc, check to see whether he's a Democrat or Republican, will you?

IS THERE A DOCTOR IN THE HOUSE?

Any schoolchild can recite the names of the great doctors: Hippocrates, Kildare, Welby. Doctors occupy a special place in society. They command respect. Hence, when their deeds are trumpeted in the local newspaper, we pay close attention.

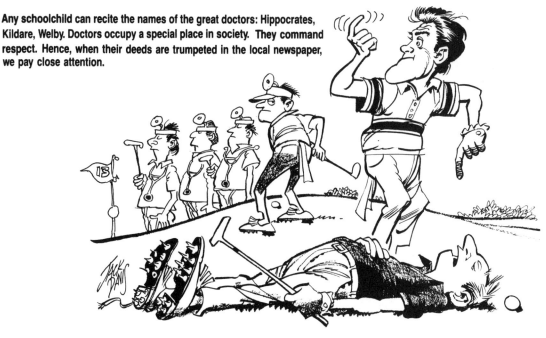

"Could you please pay in advance" department:

Doctors offer suicide guide

From staff and wire reports

BOSTON — Doctors can ethically help terminally ill patients commit suicide by prescribing sleeping pills or other drugs and telling them what dose will end their lives, a panel of prominent doctors concludes.

In recognition of National Prostate Cancer Week, Stamford urologists **RUDY T. ANDRIANI, M.D.,** and **VINCENT J. TUMINELLO, M.D.,** performed <u>free</u> rectal exams at The Stamford Hospital.

Hello, Betty? Jay. Hey, what are you doing for NPC Week next year? I've got a great idea...

Buzzards cause a buzz

Vultures make unlikely mascots at
medical building

John Everett / Chronicle

If there are vultures
at the entrance, imagine what's
waiting at the exit...

Bottled brain found in LSD apartment

A bottle marked "1 whole brain - H - 12-12-83" and containing a human brain in a fluid substance was found by a building custodian at ▓▓ N. Lake Shore Drive.

According to an 18th District Police report, a building custodian found the bottle on a shelf while cleaning out a vacated apartment. A sawed-off shotgun also was found on the premises, the report. **The bottle was taken to Lutheran General Hospital, where the brain was pronounced dead by a physician.** The discovery was made at 11 a.m. on Monday, June 19.

Of course the brain was dead. Everyone knows you have to put air holes at the top of the bottle.

State-Of-The-Art Surgery by Laser

You've seen it on television and read about it in your favorite magazine.

Now surgery by laser is available at St Clares • Riverside Medical Center.

In the hands of a skilled surgeon, it can lessen pain, reduce recovery time and save on health care costs. For everything from treating fibroid tumors to removing the gall bladder. Neurosurgery and podiatry. Gynecology and dermatology. And the list is growing daily.

If you or someone you know is considering surgery, ask your physician about the all-new Laser Center at St Clares • Riverside. Or call the Laser Center toll-free at ▓▓▓▓▓▓ for more information.

Either way, you'll learn how state-of-the-art lasers are revolutionizing surgery. And making life a little easier for all of us.

ST CLARES RIVERSIDE
MEDICAL CENTER

Pocono Road, Denville, NJ

Hey, Doc, take it easy with that laser...
Nurse, I think he's been drinking again...

Lawrence Frost, studied Custer, ingrown toenails

MONROE, Mich. — Dr. Lawrence A. Frost, a podiatrist and historian who devoted a half-century to studying the life of Gen. George Armstrong Custer, has died. He was 83.

Gee, it's too bad Custer didn't have an ingrown toenail. This guy could have saved himself a lot of research.

Dentist charged in death sent back to Va. to practice

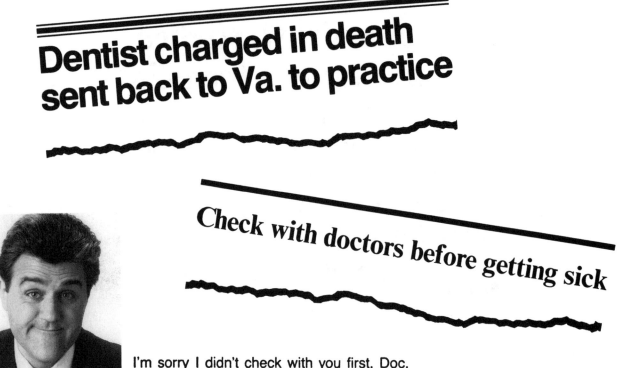

Check with doctors before getting sick

I'm sorry I didn't check with you first, Doc. I was getting a free rectal exam.

Foot doctor accused of sucking patient's toe

KEWANEE — A local podiatrist has been charged with battery and disorderly conduct for allegedly sucking the toe of a female patient and making sexually explicit comments and advances to her in his office.

Hey, it works for a snake bite.

DEATH IS JUST A STATE OF MIND

Among the most newsworthy events in any community is the passing of a loved one. Usually, it's assumed that the deceased will maintain a low profile. But as the following headlines show, the dead often have a lot of living left to do. (Out of respect for the departed, we'll offer no comment.)

Dead Man
Gets Job Back

SYDNEY, Australia (AP) — A
man who died while going to a hearing to fight his job dismissal has
been reinstated to the job.

Dead man
found in
cemetery

Dead man still goes duck hunting with pal

FARMINGTON, Ill. (AP) — Dean Goddin died in the mid-1980s, but that hasn't made him miss a single day of duck hunting with his buddy, Everett Staffeldt.

In keeping with his last request, Goddin's ashes were placed inside a pair of 2-foot mallard duck decoys that Staffeldt, a retired scientist, had originally carved for his own remains.

Tax collectors decide to leave dead man alone

OMAHA, Neb. — The IRS says it has decided not to exhume the body of an Iranian businessman who allegedly owed the government $157,000 when he died.

Dead man remains dead

CITY OF INDUSTRY, Calif.
A man apparently died while visiting a spiritual medium, who then spent a week trying to revive him, authorities said.

YOU CAN FIND IT IN THE CLASSIFIEDS

Where can you find a great buy on cellophane underwear, a job sucking the seeds out of watermelons, a lover who is ambidextrous? Why, the classifieds, of course. Take a look at these tempting offers...

BEER GUZZLING, smoking, un-
employed, Alaskan fishing guide
with black lab. seeks roommate
situation or house to rent.
12/21/W5

Please, don't everyone call at once.

Musician Wanted: Avondale Lutheran
Church is looking for a pianist for Sunday
morning worship services at 9 and 10:30
a.m. Must know how to play the piano in
Spanish. Contact (███) ███████.

Well, my specialty's Canadian, but I can get by in Spanish.

MODERATELY intelligent, occasionally nice professional male in early 40s seeks educated unencumbered woman with sense of humor & a backpack. If ex-husband in prison, please include release date.

Dear Nice Professional Man:
My husband is a beer-guzzling Alaskan fishing guide.
He'll be out of prison Thursday.
Hope to hear from you.
P.S. He'll have the backpack with him.

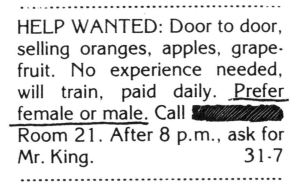

HELP WANTED: Door to door, selling oranges, apples, grapefruit. No experience needed, will train, paid daily. <u>Prefer female or male.</u> Call 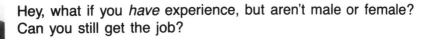 Room 21. After 8 p.m., ask for Mr. King.   31-7

Hey, what if you *have* experience, but aren't male or female? Can you still get the job?

Who says men aren't romantic?

♥♥♥♥♥♥♥♥♥♥
MIRIAM, as a token of my undying love, I'm knocking a $120 off what you still owe me. Your big Bear **WES.**
♥♥♥♥♥♥♥♥♥♥

FOUND false teeth, lower plate, good condition. Contact the Flemingsburg Sewer Plant, ■■-■■■. sept19c

Mildred, I left my false teeth on the toilet. Have you seen them?

NO EXPERIENCE NECESSARY
$35K+
WOMEN

Excel in our industry. We are a 30 year old national company.

YOU PROVIDE...

**ENTHUSIASM
PROFESSIONAL APPEARANCE
POSITIVE ATTITUDE
DESIRE TO MAKE $$**

WE PROVIDE...

**TRAINING
CONFIRMED APPTS.
50% REFERRAL BUSINESS
SEEING NEW & EXISTING ACCOUNTS
FULL BENEFITS PACKAGE**

**SOUTHWEST AREA
Mr. Daniels,** ▐▬▬▬

$35,000 *plus* women! Can I
see what they look like first?

LOST DIAPER BAG: With very sentimental items. In Taco Bell Parking Lot, Jackson. 7/8/90. Reward ███-████.

Boy, they must be *very* sentimental items.

LOST in Gotham Area. One pair of used men's underwear. Call D.J.'s Kwik Stop if found.

Lost in Gotham? Holy briefs, Batman!

FOR BETTER OR FOR WORSE

It's been said that a couple never looks more attractive than the day they're married. Perhaps it's the joy of seeing a dream fulfilled, perhaps it's the thought of all that money in the envelope from Uncle Ned. The following headlines celebrate that most sacred of institutions: marriage.

Hogg and Hamm
to Exchange Vows

Mr. and Mrs. Hugh W. Hogg of Leedey, are proud to announce the engagement and approaching marriage of their daughter, Susan Kay, to Russel G. Hamm of Weatherford. Russel is the son of Mr. and Mrs. Gene Hamm also of Weatherford.

I bet their kid's going to be a little porker.

Wong-Wright wedding plans announced

CEDAR FALLS — Announcement is being made of the engagement and approaching marriage of Siew-San Wong and Steven Wright.

Well, the nice thing is, you only need one set of monogrammed bath towels.

Associated Press

Happily married for 74 years

Sylvia Simmons, 93, and husband Ernie, 96, celebrated their 74th wedding anniversary at a Colorado Springs nursing home over the weekend. The couple were married during a blizzard in Garden City, Kan., in 1916.

You know,
it's written
all over
their faces.

353

Wife regrets staying with man she killed

She regrets it? How about him?

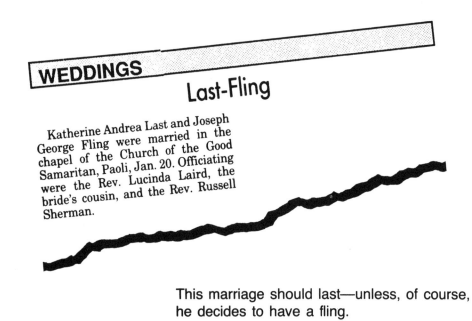

WEDDINGS

Last-Fling

Katherine Andrea Last and Joseph George Fling were married in the chapel of the Church of the Good Samaritan, Paoli, Jan. 20. Officiating were the Rev. Lucinda Laird, the bride's cousin, and the Rev. Russell Sherman.

This marriage should last—unless, of course, he decides to have a fling.

"It did seem awfully quiet on the way home" department:

Man Discovers He Left Wife At Local Station

A Texas man arrived at the home of relatives in Oklahoma City at about noon Friday to be informed he had driven away from Perry without missing his wife, leaving her at a local service station.

Woman scolded for killing husband

MOUNT CLEMENS, Mich. (AP) — A Macomb County woman received five years of probation and a scolding for stabbing her husband to death as he tried to strangle her.

"If you had an ounce of common sense in your head at all, you should have known what you were getting into," Macomb Circuit Judge Deneweth told Gay Hill, 46, at her sentencing Friday. She was also sentenced to receive mental-health counseling and told to get a job.

I tell you, if more murderers got a good scolding, there'd be less crime in this country.

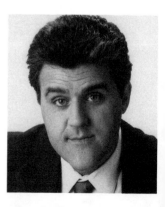

COMMUNITY AFFAIRS

Experts tell us that community spirit is built through shared activity. Potluck suppers, "Meet the Candidates" nights, gatherings where men wear funny hats and get liquored up; it's events such as these that bring us together and make for a lifestyle that can't be beat. The following headlines show just how many different types of activities Americans get involved in...

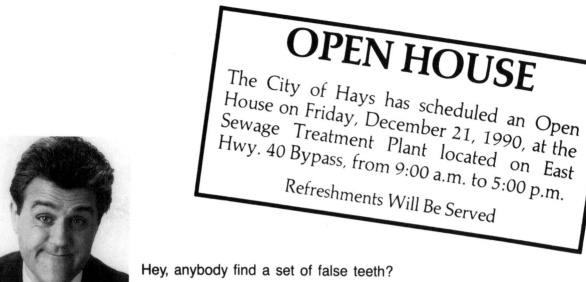

OPEN HOUSE

The City of Hays has scheduled an Open House on Friday, December 21, 1990, at the Sewage Treatment Plant located on East Hwy. 40 Bypass, from 9:00 a.m. to 5:00 p.m.

Refreshments Will Be Served

Hey, anybody find a set of false teeth?

DAUGHTER'S MEETING – All women who have served the country during the Revolution or was the mother of a patriot are invited to a coffee at 9:30 a.m. on Monday, Oct. 29 at Our Place Restaurant, First Interstate Bank Building, Carefree. The purpose of the meeting is to establish a Desert Foothills chapter of the Daughters of the American Revolution.

I hear Betsy Ross's mother will be there. It could be fun.

Civil War returns at encampment

Re-enactments of both military and civilian activities will be held. Groups of trained infantry and artillery, dressed in period costumes, will conduct military demonstrations. Other period activities will include a political debate and a church service.

There will also be presentations by the U.S. Corps of Engineers, the U.S. Sanitary Commission, and the camp chaplain Lancaster's own Maj. Gen. John F. Reynolds, the first officer killed in Gettysburg, will be on hand.

Hey, maybe we can fix him up with one of those Revolutionary War gals.

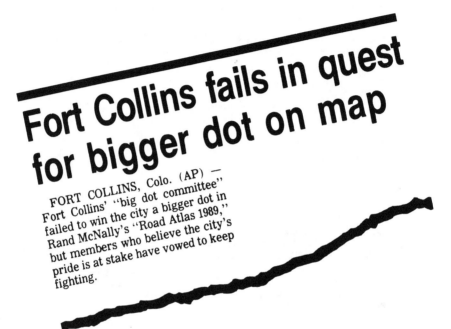

Fort Collins fails in quest for bigger dot on map

FORT COLLINS, Colo. (AP) — Fort Collins' "big dot committee" failed to win the city a bigger dot in Rand McNally's "Road Atlas 1989," but members who believe the city's pride is at stake have vowed to keep fighting.

Oh well, there's always next year.

4-H cow pie bingo to be held at Kittson County Fair

Believe me, you don't want to know.

CHRISTMAS DAY POTLUCK

December 25
Bring a dish! **KAUL FUNERAL HOME** will provide the meats. Sign up NOW, if you are interested. Registration at front counter.

11-4:00

And you thought cow-pie bingo was hard to stomach.

361

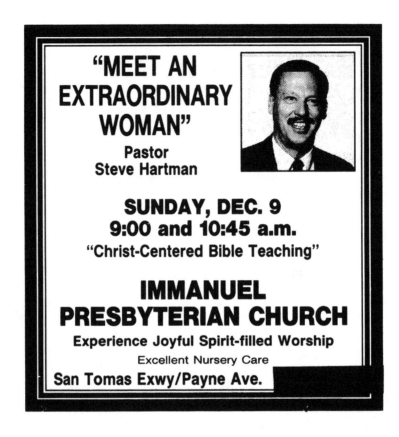

"MEET AN EXTRAORDINARY WOMAN"

**Pastor
Steve Hartman**

SUNDAY, DEC. 9
9:00 and 10:45 a.m.
"Christ-Centered Bible Teaching"

IMMANUEL
PRESBYTERIAN CHURCH

Experience Joyful Spirit-filled Worship

Excellent Nursery Care

San Tomas Exwy/Payne Ave.

Gee, just the fact that she has a mustache makes her an extraordinary woman.

NEW DOG TRAINING CLASS
10 Weeks - $25.00

SIGN-UP NIGHT
MON., JUNE 19

6:00 p.m.
At the
WAUSHARA COUNTY
FAIRGROUNDS
(By the Livestock Building)
Bring Leashes, Collars
& Shot Records
(No Dogs)
(Sponsored by Waushara
County Kennel Club)

What happens next Monday?
Just dogs, no owners?

Missouri woman big winner at hog show

Uh, lady, I wouldn't brag about this too much.

PHOTO OPPORTUNITIES

For this last chapter, I've saved my favorite photos—either those that appeared next to an unrelated headline, or those that found their way into print precisely because they were so strange. Follow me, won't you, to The Headline Gallery...

Africanized Bee threat distorted, keeper says

They travel in massive swarms devouring everything in their path with deadly stings.

That's a common notion many people have about the Africanized Honey Bee - also known as the "killer bee" - which is expected to penetrate United States borders from Mexico by 1992.

Roger Stewart, 25, of Corpus Christi holds up his cousin Andrew Canales, 3, to get a good look at the bee who represents the Reginal Transportation Au thority during the annual 16 de Septiembre Parade Sunday evening. The parade commemorated the anniversary of Mexico's independence from Spain.

Just wait till they grow to full size.

All right . . . that's it.
I'm out of here.

LEAVING AFGHANISTAN

An Afghan refugee digs a hole in front of his tent near Peshawar, Pakistan, on Thursday as the flood of refugees continued. Rebel rockets killed seven people in Kabul despite the withdrawal of Soviet troops from Afghanistan.

Troops take positions

We're looking for a few good men.

Big Roll? Looks like they're going to need a couple *Extra*-Big Rolls.

Okay, keep coming... keep coming...HOLD IT!

Developer fights for Hamilton traffic study

Wildlife Officials Working on Plan to Help Pheasants

Gene Hornbeck/World-Herald

Pheasants could prove more plentiful after a Game and Parks plan is implemented ... A final draft will be presented to the seven-member governing board of the commission for its approval in late summer or early fall.

Gee, I wonder if these are the same officials who came up with that plan to count the dead fish by poisoning the rivers. (See page 257.)

WINTRY RIDE — An Amish buggy makes its way along Hawley Road just south of Scottville, last week, amid frigid temperatures and blowing snow.

MSU student launches video delivery service

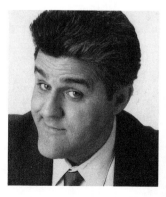

If you don't get it in thirty days or less, it's free.

Bombing range opening to public

(AP Laserphotos)

GILA BEND, Ariz. (AP) — The Air Force, Marines and a few federal agencies are putting out the welcome mat on a gunnery range twice the size of Delaware and legendary for its contradictions.

Inviting greater public use of the Barry M. Goldwater Air Force Range might appear the greatest contradiction of all: The 2.7 million-acre preserve, described as the free world's largest target range, contains seven areas where fighters strafe and bomb simulated trains, convoys and missile bases. It has three more for practicing aerial dogfights.

An information packet which includes an agreement absolving the military of any harm to the visitor refers to unexploded ordnance dating back to the 1940s and warns that "munitions items are designed to maim and kill."

Put off by the crowds at Disney World? Bored by the serenity of Yosemite? Why not put a little duck-and-cover into your backpacking?

371

Homeless live out Cinderella fantasy

President and Barbara Bush danced during an inaugural ball Friday at the Washington Convention Center.

Okay, you pretend you're the president and I'll pretend I'm the first lady...

Stay with me, Raisa, and I'll get you nylons, chocolates, and toilet paper.

President Bush leads Raisa Gorbachev by the arm as Barbara Bush and Soviet President Gorbachev assemble for a group photograph Saturday at Camp David. The group was scheduled to spend the day at the mountain retreat.

Americans grab summit opportunities

"Airline passengers sick of being treated like cattle" department:

Nosed off plane, 'smelly' pair sues airline

Associated Press

WATERTOWN, N.Y. — A couple kicked off a USAir flight after an attendant complained they smelled bad are asking the airline for an apology and the price of two of its most expensive tickets.

"Personally, I don't think we smelled any different than anybody else on the plane," Randi ~~Freeman~~ said Tuesday. She

I don't know how you play it, I don't care how you play it, and I don't want to see anyone else play it.

FOR SALE
NEEDS WORK

Ah, a little paint here,
a little plaster there...

Custom Home
FOR SALE
CALL

ILM Properties & Land Development, Inc.

Courier-Post photo by Evangelos Dousmanis

Let's face it,
when your family
starts growing,
you need a bigger
house.

Todd Berkey/The Tribune-Democrat

Davidsville's Main Street is a hub of activity in the village.

Oh, sure, it's busy now, but you should see it on a Sunday morning.

Give the people
what they want.

"Look, we're trying to find a better name" department:

Gee, that would look nice, wouldn't it—
a big wheel of cheese hanging over your fireplace?

"Some things are just too good to pass up" department:

Ya—uberburger!

And people wonder why
the banking industry
in this country is
falling apart.

It's up to each of us
to keep our dump neat.

Welcome to the Twilight Zone....